FROM MASS TO MISSION
Volume 2

Homilies that Inspire

Joseph A. Fata

ISBN: 978-1-69793-805-0

Cover art by Joseph A. Fata
Cover graphic design by
CCA Graphics (Youngstown, Ohio)

Printed in the United States of America (2019)
by Kindle Direct Publishing
First Edition, First Printing

*Scripture references are taken from
the New American Bible.*

For further information contact
St. Luke Catholic Church
5235 South Avenue
Boardman, Ohio 44512
330-782-9783

To my parents, Natale and Carmel Fata,
and all who have sustained and inspired me.

"All shall be well…
for there is force of love
moving through the universe
that holds us fast and will never let us go."

—Blessed Julian of Norwich

CONTENTS

FOREWORD

"The idea is to write it so that people hear it and it slides through the brain and goes straight to the heart."

—Maya Angelou

In Joe's last weeks, preparing his book of poems and reflections, "Chronology of a Life Well Loved," consumed much of his energy, passion, and imagination. Most of the content of "Chronology" had never been shared publicly, and I think he knew the impact it would have on those he was about to leave behind, and he hoped, on an even wider audience who may never have known him. That book, much like Volume 1 of "Mass to Mission," has given so many of us the chance to "hear" his voice, often at times when we most need to be challenged, inspired or consoled.

Joe also talked about a second volume of homilies (to be published only *after* we finished bringing "Chronology" to print, he always clarified), to offer some of his best homilies written after the publication of Volume 1, and to share some of his earlier favorites that weren't included in the first book. We organized this volume a little differently, according to the liturgical year rather than thematically. While not every Sunday and holy day was available or is included, this book reflects the movement of the church through both sacred seasons and ordinary time; it traces our salvation history and invites us into the Paschal Mystery; and most of all, it reminds us what it means to be a Eucharistic people.

My hope for this volume is as Joe's always was for his spoken and written word: that it indeed "goes straight to the heart" and that we find sparks of insight and moments of grace that lead us closer to God, to our best selves, and to a better church.

Brigid Kennedy

PREFACE

"The world is charged with the grandeur of God.
It will flame out like shining from shook foil…"

—Gerard Manley Hopkins, *God's Grandeur*

For me, a homily is about challenging while lifting up. It is about grounding while inspiring. It is about being open to the Spirit while facing the sometime harsh realities of life. It is never simply about teaching in an academic sense but always about growth at every level of our humanity and spirituality.

The homilies and reflections in this book were intended to be preached in the context of the Eucharist, the most basic and *Catholic* thing we do. Hence, they presume a certain level of faith development while at the same time calling, both preacher and hearer, to new depth, new understanding, new life.

The contents of this book have been inspired and influenced by family and friends, teachers and mentors, poets and theologians, celebrities and so-called nobodies, great literature and the daily news, people of faith and even non-believers. I have "stolen" ideas from Thomas Aquinas and Thomas Merton, Gerard Manley Hopkins and Dylan Thomas, John XXIII and Pope Francis I, Francis of Assisi and Catherine of Siena, Richard Rohr, many of you and countless others.

I appreciate the *push* from the people of St. Luke Parish to pursue this endeavor and I am grateful for their work in pulling the effort together.

It is my prayer that any inspiration you gain from this book will be a trigger for a life of learning, loving and serving.

Father Joseph A. Fata
Volume 1 Preface

ADVENT & CHRISTMAS SEASON

Jesus is calling us to pay attention to the signs of God's presence in our midst. Sometimes we are not ready to see those signs. More often, they are shrouded in holy darkness. We are not always ready to "stand erect and raise our heads" to see the beauty or the brokenness around us. We need to look deeper, more intently. Sometimes we must peer out of our own darkness to embrace these signs. We need to see beyond ourselves.

Advent is a kind of schizophrenic time. We are bombarded with flashing lights and ubiquitous music, rushing people and snarled traffic. Yet we feel a need for some peaceful darkness and quiet time. Pay attention to that need.

In spite of the busy-ness of this time of year, Advent is, first of all, a time to settle comfortably into the natural darkness, embrace some quiet and look with more than our eyes. We need to look with our hearts and souls in order to really "see" our world as God offers it. With that in mind, I was reflecting, mostly for myself. But I offer this reflection to you as a kind of invitation into the Advent season:

I remember…when streetlights weren't so bright.
They didn't turn night into day.
From rippled, hanging saucers,
the bulbs cast white circles on the pavement below.
It was better then.
You could run from white spot to white spot.
But if you liked, you could hide in the dark spaces,
feeling safe, knowing the light was close by.
Ironically, you could see the world
more clearly from the darkness
once your eyes and heart adjusted.
I remember…when mothers didn't need cellphones
to text you home.
A yell from the back door was more than enough.
It was better then.

1

When darkness fell and it was time to go,
you could always linger for a moment or two,
comfortable in the shadows of dusk.
(She called it dawdling.)
You could look back on the freedom of the day
knowing that the morning light would bring more of the same.

I remember...the big culvert in Lincoln Park.
We thought it was a tunnel
where spies and commies used to hide out.
I could stand up straight and run and jump
and not hit my head.
It was better then (before I was too big).
We could hide there
and when we weren't yelling for one another,
we could be quiet in the darkness and never be afraid.
You knew your friends were close
even if you couldn't see them.
With pen knives and string and other objects
pilfered from dad's workbench,
you would protect each other
and always make it to the light at the other end.

Now the dark places in our lives are of a different sort.
Maybe more scary, maybe not.
But from that darkness,
if you let it settle,
you can still see the world more clearly.
You can still linger for a moment
and feel the freedom of the day.
You can hide and be quiet
knowing your friends are close.
So embrace the darkness
(or let it embrace you).
Look backward or forward, it doesn't matter.
It all seems clearer from the darkness
where God, the eternal light is waiting.

God wanted a very ordinary young girl to be the mother of Jesus. He didn't want her to be a queen or a princess or living in a palace or ruling over lots of people. But she had to be a good person…holy and familiar with God's history among her people.

Jesus would have to be one just like us. And so, his mother had to be just like us.

Mary's life was pretty much laid out before her by her family and her culture. Her life would be simple, hidden, uncomplicated.

But God interrupts her pre-ordered life. God asks Mary to surrender the life expected of her. He entrusts her with the child who will be the Light of the World, the Word of God. And Mary says yes because in her simplicity and holiness she understands her life is a gift, and the only way to say thanks to God is to say yes to unexpected interruption.

God often interrupts our lives also. We might not be able to live the simple, well-ordered life we wish. God's messenger Gabriel appears to us in the needs of our children, the struggles of our families and friends, the cries of the poor, the despair of those who are lost or marginalized. We are called to bring God's Christ into our Bethlehems, our divided and broken world.

Today we celebrate Mary. And we remember that we too are called to welcome God's messenger and say yes to the interruptions that call us to a deeper relationship with God.

Second Sunday of Advent (C)
Luke 3:1-6

"A baptism of repentance." Many people, if not most, don't really know what that even means. Repentance is NOT about feeling sorry; it is not about guilt or regret. The word repentance, as used by John in the original Greek means CHANGE—not just feeling sad but resolving to DO something.

So here comes Christmas. For some people, on any given day, it is just another headache on your already packed schedule. Another layer of places to go and things to do and expectations to meet. The schedules posted on your iPhone calendar or your refrigerator door are already a nightmare. When will it all get done?! If the stress is getting the better of you, it is time to REPENT.

CHANGE, CHANGE, CHANGE the way you go about the day. Do less instead of more. Be quiet.

Maybe there is a sadness hanging over the coming holiday. A relationship you're feeling badly about or an awkward situation that needs attention or words between you and someone that are a source of bitterness. There is a chasm somewhere. So…consider REPENTING.

CHANGE, CHANGE, CHANGE. Listen to some quiet music. Make a phone call. Don't text; rather, let them hear your voice. Build a bridge.

Is there a certain emptiness you're feeling? Maybe you're tired and just going through motions. Maybe someone is not coming home, something is out of your control. Could you possibly bring joy where there is sadness? Could you bring hope where cynicism is holding sway? Start with REPENTANCE.

CHANGE, CHANGE, CHANGE. Do something for someone who can't pay you back. Break free of the anger that is shriveling you. Speak only positive words today.

Who among us is not brought down by recent events that depress our holiday spirit? Paris, San Bernardino. Feelings of anger, fear. All the Christmas carols in the world can't take away the bad feelings. Could it be time to REPENT?

4

CHANGE, CHANGE, CHANGE. Pray. Act. Free yourself from the desire for revenge. Look to the Peace of Christ. Don't let terror, fear and anger take away your best self...the self that has Christ for a brother. Avoid conversations that speak of retaliation. Speak words of peace.

Repentance indeed. Don't just feel bad, do something. Change can't happen, in your heart or in the world, if we believe there is no reason to change. Change is not part of anyone's perfect image of Christmas.

Repentance begins with the acknowledgement that everything isn't fine. (In here...or out there.) Repentance begins with the acknowledgement that "Christmas as usual" won't make us happy, the acknowledgement that we have all been blown off course, that the geography of our lives is filled with crooked roads and steep mountains. (Again, in here and out there.)

Make this a season of real repentance: change, recapture the serenity of Christmas, repair the broken relationship, restore the meaning of Christ's birth for all people of the world, even the ones who don't believe. Embrace generosity and quiet and peace. In the spirit of John the Baptizer, make a new, straight path for God to enter your heart and your world.

Today is traditionally called Gaudete Sunday. It is the pink candle Sunday. Gaudete means rejoice. But it is probably beyond anyone's memory when we could gather free of all distress and worry and truly rejoice. There is always something looming, always something to drown our joy.

Many of you are old enough to remember Debbie Downer of *Saturday Night Live* fame. She could walk into any happy situation and immediately turn it sour with the look on her face and the signature "Wah Wah" of a muted trumpet. In many ways, all of life could be viewed as a Debbie Downer experience. That is why she was so funny...because it was a parody of someone we knew, or maybe ourselves.

Life continues to issue challenges to true joy. The season's first "nor'easter" blew chilling rains and ice into our world. In multiple cities, nightly protests reminded us of racial conflicts not yet resolved. Violence is sustained in the Middle East. There is plenty to bring us down. "Gaudete? Rejoice? Who is kidding who?" And yet, as disciples of Jesus we DO rejoice. And we must! Without naiveté, with holy daring and blessed boldness, in the face of what seems like deepening darkness, we light a third candle in the Advent wreath evoking the dawning of the Day of the Lord. And hoping against hope, we hear today's Gospel and know that what the Pharisees were asking John are really questions aimed at us: "Who are you? What are you? What do you have to say for yourself?"

Couldn't we make Isaiah's "job description" for God's servant, our own job description? To bring glad tidings...instead of forwarding that nasty email that parades as humor. To heal the brokenhearted...instead of looking for excuses to relieve the guilty of responsibility. To proclaim liberty to captives...instead of parading our self-righteousness as reality. To announce a year of favor...instead of seeing everyday as a personal attack on "MY" happiness. Yes, today we rejoice, not because of what we have done or not done, but because of what we are called to be: people "robed with salvation, wrapped in justice."

6

This 4th Sunday of Advent is all about Mary. It is true that the first reading is about the Messianic promise and the House of David. But we'll get back to that. It still ends up being about Mary.

Barbara Brown Taylor is an author, a teacher and an Episcopal minister. She has given me a great idea. She keeps a small box on her dresser in front of two icons, one of Jesus and one of the Virgin Mary. When people ask her to pray for them, she writes their name on a slip of paper and puts it in the box.

Taylor writes that she has great confidence in entrusting her prayers to the Mother of Jesus. She says, "Mary is more like me than her son is, after all. Both of Mary's parents were human. She was born, lived and died in usual ways. What was unusual about her was her reliability. No matter what life pitched at her, Mary did not duck. She endured a difficult pregnancy to bear a singular child, whom she loved reliably through all the years of his controversial life. When her son was cut down, she was there. When it came time to prepare his body, she was there. When he was not in his tomb, she was there. As much as I hate to presume on her reliability, I know she will remember the people whose names I have placed in the brass box, even when I forget."

Taylor is quite on target, no doubt. Mary's entire life was a series of annunciations—God constantly calling her to be the reflection of his compassion, to be a source of persevering faith, to mirror in her motherhood of the Christ, God's loving providence for all his children.

God asks that same reliability of all of us in the everyday living of our own lives. But, alas, that reliability is often absent. In fact, if I had to identify the top five problems in our culture today, the lack of reliability would be right up there.

Many people are so self-absorbed, so focused on fulfilling their own shallow needs, so blind to the ones closest to them, so intent on controlling others, they have forgotten how to be reliable.

Mary's experience is like our own. It is not easy to be reliable.

7

You get tired. Discerning God's will demands time and THOUGHTFULNESS. In God's annunciations to us, we end up with a great deal to process, to sort out, if we are paying attention. Only with Mary's reliable faith and trust can we survive, let alone make God's presence known in our time and place. Is what you are doing in your life making God's presence known? Is what you are doing for your children making God's presence known? Is your interaction with the world making God's presence known? If not, do something else. Be reliable. Be open to the presence of Gabriel announcing that the Lord is with us, that we have nothing to fear, that we have been called by God to "give birth" to his Son.

Back to that first reading: God promised to establish a kingdom like no other. Who could have known the promise would be fulfilled through a young girl's reliability? Most of the world missed it. But Mary didn't. And neither will we.

"Silent night, holy night/ all is calm, all is bright..."

A holy night to be sure in Bethlehem. But hardly silent and anything but calm. We have so romanticized and gilded the Christmas mystery that we miss a crucial point in all of it: God reaching out for us in spite of our chaos.

That night in Bethlehem was anything but silent. The night would have been shattered by the blood-curdling cries of wild animals in the unfriendly hillsides. In a cold dark cave where livestock huddled for warmth and protection, a young, frightened woman gives birth to her child, while her carpenter-husband stands by trying to keep things together. Finally, amid the bleating of those sheep and the braying of other animals, the sound of a newborn's first cries for life add to the cacophony smothering out stillness.

That so-called "silent night" was filled with terror, pain, cold and bone-numbing exhaustion. You know how it is when you are anxious. You can't sleep anyway. Mary's thoughts were no doubt racing. And Joseph's fitful dreams had precluded much sleep for him anyway.

And there was no "silence," no calm for anyone that night in crowded, chaotic Bethlehem. At that point, remember, there were no Christmas celebrations. It was business as usual. Plus, the town was bursting at the seams with travelers there for Caesar's great census. And the reason for the census was disturbing in itself: so Caesar could exact more unjust taxes and get conscripts for his devastating army marching across the landscape of the known world to cower people in subjection.

There was no calm in all of Israel—only tension and conflict between the Jewish people and their Roman occupiers. Palestine of the first century was hardly a place of "heavenly peace." It was a land torn apart by oppression, poverty, violence in the streets, and terror. Sound familiar? And that's the crucial point again. God doesn't need political peace or even an imposed silence. Dictators can do that.

And so, is this homily about ruining your Christmas? You know better than that. It is about getting the real picture so that manufactured memory and sweet nostalgia don't blot out the stunning story of a simple Jewish girl giving birth to God himself. It is true, there was no calm, no silence.

And yet…and yet, on that noisy, chaotic, anxious night Christ WAS born. Hidden in a very unheavenly, dark cave, veiled in humanness, the light of Christ dawned. Amid the pain and anguish of a devastated people, Christ came with hope and transforming joy.

Silence and calm are not external props for a Christmas pageant. Silence is a place you choose to go because you know God will speak to you there. Calm is a choice you make in spite of the terror, technology and materialism of a world gone mad. Peace is a gift that comes even in turmoil.

God still comes to transform our own dark nights, chaos and pain into holy nights of peace. Amid the noise and clamor that consume us, the voice of God can whisper in the silence of the hearts we have prepared.

If that first Christmas had been calm, quiet and peaceful, we wouldn't be saved. It had to be our own kind of world that was saved. God did not redeem us by creating a contrived silence and an external peace. He redeemed us in an imperfect world with a confused man, a fearful woman, a crying baby and a group of other players no one would expect. It can happen for us too. Find the silence within. Bring Christ to the chaos. Make peace.

Addendum: God intends Christmas to be an entire lifetime relationship. But because we fill it with constant chatter, busy-ness and chaos, it remains only a day, because that's all we can handle. Embrace the silence, experience the possibilities. *(From Richard Rohr's Christmas meditation, 2014)*

Christmas (Midnight Mass, 2015)
Luke 2:1-14

You may not know it, but the Gospel just proclaimed is not the only one recommended for Christmas, even though it is the one we hear most often. No, the Church actually offers four Gospel options:

1. The one we just heard from Luke about Caesar's decree and Mary and Joseph's trip to Bethlehem.
2. Then there is the one from Matthew that gives the genealogy of Jesus and focuses on Joseph's dilemma.
3. There is another from Luke that focuses on the aftermath, how the shepherds spread good news and how Mary kept all these things in her heart.
4. And then the fourth option is from John's Gospel. It is about Jesus being the Word made flesh and the light of the world.

It is too bad we can't hear them all. There is so much to ponder…more than the trappings and distractions of Christmas allow. So, I did some pondering for you. See if you can find parallels for your own life in the details of the Christmas Gospels.

—Is it enough…to respect our roots and remember where we came from?

—Is it enough…for an unwed mother to say "yes" to God's plan and bring a promise to life?

—Is it enough…for a confused man to remain faithful and loving and strong?

—Is it enough…to hold on to a dream in the face of so much negativity?

—Is it enough…to know that Caesar's decrees cannot take away our freedom?

—Is it enough…to trudge over the hills of life and keep focused on the destination?

—Is it enough…to look beyond poverty and crisis in any family?

—Is it enough…to see rocks and hills, birds and beasts and all creation as blessing and responsibility?

11

—Is it enough…to be changed just a bit so we can share what we believe?

—Is it enough…for a mother to keep things in her heart?

—Is it enough…to know that Word and Flesh are not polar opposites but one reality?

—Is it enough…to face adversity and disappointment and continue to have faith?

—Is it enough…to be overcome by deep sadness at the death of a friend?

—Is it enough…for simple people to pay attention to midnight skies and listen for angels?

—Is it enough…for men and women of stature to look for a star and leave their castles and comfort behind?

—Is it enough…to make a journey through the tall trees and under the low hanging moon to a place of birth and death?

Indeed, sometimes the celebration gets in the way of the remembering.

Think about this stunning story.

See God's hand in the details of your own Christmas story.

Turn down the lights.

Shut out the noise.

Embrace the silence.

Hold on to the Child.

Hold on to the promise.

Look for the compassion and mercy of God
and know that "it is enough."

Rabbi Lawrence Kushner offers this little snippet: A rabbi prayed to the great prophet Elijah.

"Where," the rabbi asked, "shall I find the Messiah?"

"At the gate of the city," the prophet replied.

"But how shall I recognize him?"

"He sits among the lepers," Elijah said.

"Among the lepers!" the rabbi cried. "What is he doing there?"

"He changes their bandages," Elijah replied. "He changes their bandages, one by one."

That is the true mystery of Christmas. Of course, we prefer to find the Messiah sitting in the temple, like in today's Gospel. We get that. Or we prefer to see him in the manger with shepherds and kings. That's nicer. It fits our frame of reference. Or maybe we can see and understand him forgiving a sinner or HEALING a leper, you know, like in the Gospel stories. But just changing bandages? Certainly the Messiah can accomplish greater things.

Maybe that is the most we can expect of this season of the Messiah. This is the time when families come together. Today is the feast of the Holy Family. But face it, it takes more than a festive Christmas dinner and some gifts to fix some of our families. Christmas doesn't necessarily solve all our problems or cure all our ills. Sometimes the most we can do is change bandages. That means

—having the patience to listen (even if you don't have all the answers);

—having the selflessness to forgive (even if you have been hurt);

—having the commitment to mend (even if you can't cure).

Again, that is the true mystery of Christmas: that God became one of us, lived among us, came to birth through our moments of joy and grief, despair and hope, anger and forgiveness.

Of course, we want our miracles; we want our questions answered. But there is more to it. Don't reduce the Messiah to a mere miracle-worker or extra-terrestrial.

Here, in the Christ Child, the sacred is not some abstract concept of theological theory. In fact, the love of God is ENFLESHED. The Word becomes a human word. The Messiah changes bandages. And sometimes all that means is that God takes on a human face. My face can bring comfort. Your face can look in love and cradle a hurting heart. My words can transform hearts. Your word can inspire. Changing bandages is not pretty work. It is not miraculous work. It takes time.

The Messiah is the one who knows our lives are filled with disappointment and sometimes pain and despair. But he enters our lives anyway and sits among us. The Messiah lived through the storms and crises we all live through.

It is all a matter of perspective and faith. Regina Brett is a *Cleveland Plain Dealer* columnist and a very well-balanced Catholic. Before Christmas she wrote an excellent article about all that nonsense that some Christians spout about how some people and non-Christians are trying to hijack Christmas and eliminate Christ from the picture. Such people are obsessed by negativity. They see anti-Christian conspiracies behind everything. And they become these mindless evangelists preaching their own gospel. Basically Ms. Brett said: Fear not the people who say, "Seasons Greetings" or "Happy Holidays." They are not the enemy. Don't worry about Santa Claus or snowmen replacing Jesus. Christ is never going to get lost as long as believers continue to do more than set up manger scenes and sing Happy Birthday to Jesus.

But you see (as Richard Rohr reminds us), the ultimate disguise whereby you can remain a mean-spirited, judgmental person is to do it for God or country. Ours is not a Messiah who came to strike down all the non-believers and reward the ones we deem to be worthy and to work our pre-determined miracles.

Changing bandages. That is what will keep Christ in Christmas. That is what the Messiah is doing. He does it on his own and in us. It is a little different than we thought.

Mary, Mother of God
New Year's Day (2015)
Luke 2:16-21

For most of us, Christmas is the marker for family and personal histories: a child's first Christmas; the first Christmas after she died; the Christmas he was away in Iraq; the first Christmas in our new house; his last Christmas with us.

It's a mixed bag, isn't it? Most memories are comforting and happy. But some are painful. The Christmas someone came home. The Christmas someone left. But they are memories nonetheless, and they make us who we are.

This New Year's Day, we remember how Mary kept all those things, reflecting on them in her heart. And we do too.

This New Year's Day, one week after Christmas, shepherds are back. And what did they see? A mother, a father, a baby. All very ordinary. But they saw something extraordinary too: the very face of God. But they could only see it through the eyes of faith.

This New Year's Day, we open our eyes of faith and see.

With eyes of faith you can look back and look forward.

Memories are important. We learn from them…we are formed by them…we are inspired by them. The future is important too, obviously.

This New Year's Day, we remember that God uses every event (past and present and future), every person (gone before us and with us now). God uses it all as an opportunity to draw us closer to himself.

This New Year's Day we stand on the edge of 2015, looking for the face of God, knowing it will be revealed in unexpected ways.

It is not news to tell you that we live in a time of opportunity and peril. On one hand, there is the widening gap between the rich and poor, the hunger that stalks our earth, the pollution of our environment that threatens our very lives. On the other hand, there are technological and scientific advances, new medical treatments which stop the spread of disease, extension of human life, incredible communication possibilities. What does the future hold?

Two brothers in a small African village were about to set out to make their fortune. "Go with my blessing," their father said, "but on your way put marks on the trees lest you lose your way."

The brothers went off. The older one proceeded through the thick forest. As he went, he cut down some trees and carved distinguishing marks into others so as to differentiate between his marks and the marks of others.

The younger brother took a different route. As he journeyed, he stopped at various houses and villages along the way and offered to work in return for food and shelter. He returned his host's kindness with generosity and gratitude. He made many friends along the way.

When the two brothers returned home, they shared their adventures with their father. Happy to have his sons back, their father said, "I would like to see the marks you left." So, he went off with the one son. He observed the fallen trees and distinguishing markings he left.

Then he went with the other son. They were received warmly by all the friends his son had made, a clear trail of friendship, gratitude and kindness. The father and son returned home with many gifts and warm memories.

Today's feast of Epiphany is not only a story of three wise men and their search for the Christ Child; it is a paradigm for our journey through life. No matter how insignificant one's life may seem, it is a journey through time in which we seek the Christ and leave clear marks of our route.

What does the future hold? Who knows? The Magi saw a star they had not seen before. They believed, and they searched. Their journey speaks of the yearning of the human heart to find a higher wisdom, to find a brighter light. Why settle for the popular wisdom? Haven't you figured out it doesn't work? Why settle for the typical shadows and gloom? Haven't you figured out that is a dead end? Like the Magi and King Herod, we can make choices that alter our future.

What does the future hold? Of course, it is shrouded in mystery. Like the three wise men in the Gospel, we may have to change course and proceed on a different way. As long as we leave gifts, not measured by weight or arbitrary value, but gifts that are symbolic of what we believe and the One we seek, we can be sure we, in turn, will have many gifts and warm memories when we return home.

Today celebrates not only the Epiphany of Christ in our world but also the grace for each of us to be a constant Epiphany of recreating and transforming our lives in the Love of Emmanuel, God with us.

They have always fascinated us, these travelers who must have loomed at the entrance of the cave before, and astonished and probably alarmed Mary and Joseph.

The Magi do not fit into that tiny world of villagers and stables and sheepherders. Their sophistication clashes with the simplicity they discover. Their power and affluence highlight the vulnerability of a child and a displaced family. They are urban, affluent and cosmopolitan in a world that is rural, poor and provincial.

We recognize a deep wisdom that we respect even if we do not share. They paid their respects to Herod, but had the wisdom to see him as genocidal, a mental wreck in spite of his superficial power. We respect them because they were not willing (as we often are!) to sell their souls and compromise their morals simply to be associated with what the world sees as successful and powerful. They would not have wasted their time pursing the sham of celebrity and fame, the very things that obsess so many of us. They were searching for meaning, not merely entertainment. Every journey must be more than just a vacation.

We like these men who represent the wisdom that recognizes human life as a journey in search of One who calls us beyond ourselves into faithful service, who calls us out of our limited little worlds into the heart of something greater than ourselves, who challenges us to offer the best of our gifts, even if they are not treasures of gold.

We admire these mysterious characters who could kneel with supreme grace and dignity before vulnerability and poverty. This is what makes them "wise"—that they could see the glory that is hidden in a humble place and a little child. We are drawn to that.

They were willing to go to the peripheries long before Saint Francis of Assisi and Pope Francis of Argentina reminded us that it is a universal call. We like that.

But we are called to more than just liking or admiring or being impressed with these characters. For us, like them, it is what we do after we leave Bethlehem that is the measure of our sincerity. The proclamation of the deacon reminds us that it is "what comes next" that matters. It is the continuing of the journey that determines our future.

I read the poem "The Journey of the Magi" every year. At the conclusion of the poem, T.S. Eliot cuts to the heart of the gospel message when he has one of the Magi musing:

"All this was a long time ago, I remember,
And I would do it again, but set down
This set down
This: were we led all that way for
Birth or Death? There was a Birth, certainly,
We had evidence and no doubt. I had seen birth and death,
But had thought they were different; this birth was
Hard and bitter agony for us, like Death, our death.
We returned to our places, these Kingdoms,
But no longer at ease here, in the old dispensation,
With an alien people clutching their gods.
I should be glad of another death."

Like the Magi, we leave Bethlehem and head into the year that stretches before us. Will our journey have changed us? Will our future be different?

Baptism of the Lord (2015)
Mark 1:7-11

Matthew, Mark and Luke all include the event of Christ's Baptism in their Gospels. Matthew and Luke both describe the heavens being opened. Mark's imagery today is much more intense. He says, "On coming up out of the water, Jesus saw the heavens being TORN OPEN!"

"Torn open" decisively declares God's definitive in-breaking into human history and into the "ordinary time" of your life and mine. In spite of the strong imagery, only Jesus seems to have seen the heavens being torn open, seems to have heard the voice calling him beloved. Remember, Mark wasn't there. He is proclaiming, years later, what he believed about Jesus. So, this was a definitive turning point in the life of Jesus as he went public with his mission.

For Jesus and for Mark, the heavens being "torn open" was the conviction that those heavens, which had been long sealed off from the children of earth, were now opened as God presents his son. That is why Jesus had to "descend into hell" as we say, so as to lift to heaven all those who had been shut out by sin until sin was overcome by the Resurrection. Up to the time of Jesus' Baptism, there was only occasional contact through messengers and prophets and symbols.

Now there was a living person who could show us the face of God, not just deliver a message or prophecy.

But as always, today isn't just about the Baptism of Jesus. It is also about us. So, what about us? Could the heavens be "torn open" in our lives too? Or is that just Bible imagery from a by-gone day? I don't think so. God continues to break into our lives. Remember, only we need to see it. And it could be as quiet as a knock on the door. It could be as subtle as the heavenly voice in our heart. It could be as unremarkable as a quiet conversation with a friend or a stranger. It could be as gentle as the bright look on the face of one of those babies we welcome into the Church on their Baptism.

20

Remember, God can break in however he chooses. It doesn't have to be a cataclysmic event. It doesn't even have to be something positive. Sometimes the "tearing open" can be something or someone we would otherwise avoid. It could be a fact we are denying. It could be a peaceful joy or an exuberant celebration. It can be a silent sadness or a cry of mourning. It can be a quiet hurting or a healing touch. The very thing that seems to be disrupting your life can be the process that moves you to a brighter future.

Don't wallow around in your shut-up cocoon with your heavens sealed closed. Don't dig in your heels. Don't sell yourself or God short. Look for the "tearing open" of the heavens in your life. You don't have to be spoon-fed. You don't need me or anyone else to identify it. Open your eyes, open your heart. Believe that the Father can "tear open" your heavens. Believe it can happen in many ways. Watch for it. Be open to it. However it comes, when you are unselfish and generous, it will always end in the assurance that you are indeed a beloved child, pleasing to God.

ORDINARY TIME, PART 1

Second Sunday in Ordinary Time (C)
John 2:1-11

Today's Gospel, today's miracle, is a fitting FIRST sign of what Jesus was sent by God to do: to transform our world from the brokenness of sin and deadness of poverty into God's banquet table of generosity, hope, healing and forgiveness.

But if Mary and that couple and all their guests had simply focused on the negative, nothing good would have happened. Those jars would have remained empty. THEY would have remained empty.

So it is with us. If all we do is focus on my hurt, my anger, my embarrassment, my problem…whatever…then we will be like empty dried up wine jars. We all know people like that. We all can be people like that. Shriveled up, hopeless, empty. Looking for a reason to be disappointed. Expecting the worst. Maintaining emptiness.

You all know, if you are stingy and miserly, you can't see God's abundance. If you carry smallness and hatred in your heart, it has a negative impact on all your relationships. If you focus on the empty wine jars, you will never drink of God's miracles.

In Christ, the watered-down wine of fear and self-centeredness is replaced with

—the "new wine" of compassion and gratitude for the life God has given us;

—the new wine of honor and respect for every human being;

—the new wine of justice and mercy.

But we need to give it a chance. We need to invite Jesus in. That's how it began with that couple in Cana. In fact, that's how it began with Mary herself. She invited God into her life. No miracle can happen when we clench our fists, stop up our ears and seal off our heart.

It is no accident that Jesus' ministry begins with a party overflowing with wine, filled with abundance and happy people. When did our life in Christ become somber, solemn and boring?

23

Ministry is obviously about keeping the party going. Who ever said there is room at God's feast for exclusion and empty jars? It is always about openness and abundance.

We talk a lot about evangelization. Evangelization is about no one going home empty and sad. We talk about having faith. Faith itself is about believing that Jesus can transform our lives into the rich wine of love and compassion.

We cannot domesticate this Gospel into a neat story about some nice couple who invite a holy man to their wedding. It is about what Richard Rohr calls the scandal of the Incarnation. That is, it is about a God who becomes so human that he cannot remain separated from our sadness or our joy. In this case, he comes to the party, keeps it going and transforms us in the process.

Third Sunday in Ordinary Time (A)
Matthew 4:12-23

The Gospel is certainly about vocation and letting go. It is about hearing the call and letting go of our own nets to follow Jesus who will provide us with other nets. It is about letting go of our anxieties and fears…letting go of our selfishness and our need to control…letting go of the things that tie us down and tie us up…even letting go of our plans so that God's plan can grow in us. It's vocation and letting go.

Christ didn't just call those fishermen on the shore of Galilee. He is calling us too. Calling us to abandon the nets that we think are so important even though they will never catch what we want anyway. Yet, we hang on to whatever we think we have that's providing ourselves with only false security.

The noted psychologist Abraham Maslow contends that, essential to every healthy personality and good life is a sense of mission and purpose. We call it vocation. And every healthy vocation means letting go of something.

Lewis Moll has written a poem entitled "Flying Kites" that tells a story about a little boy and his father who spend hours putting together an old-fashioned kite with pinewood slats and delicate paper. They fashion a tail of rags strung together. Then like bold conquerors they march out into a windy day, father and son, to let fly their kite of dreams. Dad instructs the boy to hold the string tight and run as fast as he can. After a few false starts and frustrated attempts, the kite is airborne. And the boy is in control as the dad shows him how to let out the string little by little. And the kite flies higher and higher. The boy seems mesmerized. Then, to his father's surprise the boy lets go of the string and jumps up and down in sheer delight as the kite, free of its tether, soars higher and higher until it is only a speck in the distance. And the boy is not sad that his kite is free to fly.

Walking home together, the father realizes that he will too soon have to loosen the tie that binds him to his son and let the boy go to make his own place in the world. After all, all of life is about letting go. And the father wonders if he will release the string as unselfishly as the boy did.

And so, Christ calls each of us to let go, right now, of the things that keep us from being, in the words of the Gospel, "fishers of men."

Christ will give us whatever we need, in whatever ocean and on whatever shore we find ourselves.

—In our own poverty, he gives us the nets and the words to fish for those who are in need.

—In our own pain, he calls us to catch and comfort those who suffer.

—In our own despair and loss, he shows us how to fish for those who have lost hope.

—In our own doubts, he gives us the net to catch those whose faith is weak.

—In our own floundering, he gives us the gift to find those who are lost.

—In our own ignorance, he gives us the wisdom to share faith with those who need it.

—In our own hard-heartedness, he gives us the gentleness to reach out to others.

No, today's Gospel isn't just about Peter and Andrew and James and John. It is about you and me being willing to let go of whatever it is that holds us back and go out there and reel in anyone who hasn't heard Christ's voice calling them yet. It is about you and me diving deep into the waters of a relationship with Christ, so that every person we touch will feel the fire of a love that knows how to let go and say "Yes."

Third Sunday in Ordinary Time (B)
Mark 1:14-20

Most of us would not claim to live exciting or stimulating lives. Life can be pretty humdrum. Many feel their existence is somehow imposed upon them and they have no power over it. I must do this job…I have these responsibilities…I'm stuck with this or that situation…I never get a break…same old thing day in and day out. In my opinion, one of the most serious diseases threatening our Western culture is boredom. People are of dying of it.

Yet many opportunities arise each day that afford us no second chance. We miss them. They are lost opportunities. Lost because people fail to respond. Lost because people procrastinate.

They are opportunities for renewal, opportunities for connections, opportunities for growth, opportunities for happiness. And people miss them every day. Specifically, our God has a history of placing opportunities before his people. Granted, those opportunities are often veiled in negatives.

Our Scripture readings today give us examples of people who seized the moment in choosing the path of life: Jonah and the Ninevites. Jonah was hard-headed, closed and didn't want to adjust his thinking, resisting the invitation to do the right thing. When he finally did his life changed. It was, as Scripture scholars joke, a whale of an opportunity.

The Ninevites were the classic case of being hard-hearted, lost and hopeless. At least, that is what the Israelites thought. But when they repented their whole existence changed.

The call of the Apostles was another blessed opportunity. Their response probably didn't change the externals of their lives that much. But it changed their attitude. It gave them new vision. It rekindled the dying embers of their hope.

What opportunities are you missing? God continues to place them before you. Why do you resist? Why do you dig in your heels? One small change could give your life new purpose and new meaning. We are called to seize the moment.

Today is the day to love your spouse. Today is the opportunity to give your children guidance. Now is the time to visit a sick friend, to comfort someone who is grieving, to think beyond your pride and your own selfish needs, to pull back from the edge of boredom.

With our God, the very thing you are resisting could be the threshold to an opportunity. With Jesus, the call is always to new life, even when it seems the exact opposite.

Jesus calls us to abandon our "fishing nets" of self-interest and seek instead, happiness and fulfillment for others. Jesus and his disciples probably never traveled more than 50 miles from home, yet he shows them (and us) a bigger world than our own little Galilees. He invites us into that bigger world of generosity, forgiveness and reconciliation. It is a world of no borders and immense freedom.

Fourth Sunday in Ordinary Time (C)
Luke 4:21-30

Jesus was speaking prophetically today. And he knew that was dangerous. I am sure, from the human perspective, Jesus liked it when people "were amazed at the gracious words that came from his mouth." But he had to know, at some level, that they might reject him if he spoke too much truth…that many would find his words too much to swallow.

Face it, it is very difficult to be a prophetic voice. And he must have felt that he might need to "pass through their midst" before they would "get it." Prophets have always run into problems. They were stoned and killed in the Old Testament. It was difficult in Jesus' time. It is difficult now, especially in our culture. But being a prophet is definitely our baptismal call. Someone must do it for all of us.

Our culture prefers it if we are politically correct or intellectually castrated or spiritually bland. But don't get me wrong, being prophetic is not the same as being offensive, mean spirited or unforgiving. And we are seeing too much of all that lately. When everybody is angry, nobody is prophetic. There is a difference.

A prophet first of all speaks the truth, and not the truth as he or she interprets it from an ego-driven mindset, but the truth. And if you are honest and sincere, you can always find out the truth. If you don't know the truth, it is best to keep your mouth shut.

But the fact is, for most of us, deep down, we do know the truth. And that truth must be spoken. You must speak it to the broken and the vulnerable. It must be spoken to the young and formative, and, most of all, the truth must be spoken to power.

Look around. Who is speaking healing and comfort to those who need it? Who is being a mentor to the young? Who is standing up to the powers that be? Prophecy is painfully absent. But if you find someone like that, affirm him or her. There is a prophet. If you can be that person, own it. The world needs you.

Parents must be prophets. Teachers must be prophets. Preachers must be prophets. Friends must be prophets. Even if it is a risk, even if you get rejected—at least for a time.

29

Allison Lobron writes for the *Boston Globe Magazine*. She talks about her toddler son. He is at the age where the world is a grand experiment and he must test everything. She says, often he will reach for the stove, knives or scissors and shout to himself "no" as he does so. Then hand hovering over the forbidden object, he will look up at his mother to see what she will do. When she says "no" along with him, he looks pleased.

She says his pleasure does not come from the boundary that has been set but from the sense that he has figured something out about how the world works. He likes it. And her voice guides him.

But, she goes on, when there is something new in his life and she says "no" his response is not positive. His response is intense and frustrated.

There are times when the prophetic voice must say "no" to what is going on in the world. And it is always time for the prophetic voice to say "yes" to what God is calling us to.

As prophets, we will often find ourselves in that difficult position of having to be "the grown up" for our children, or for adults who are acting like children. Such a prophetic stand stretches our knowledge or imagination and causes second guessing.

But to follow Jesus is to speak and act with integrity, to do what is right and just, no matter how unpopular we become. Popularity is not usually a good sign. In our day especially, the day of media untruth and media driven celebrity status, popularity is a sign of insincerity. Would that we were all unpopular. Would that we were all prophets.

30

Job is alive and well in most of us. Within the last two weeks I had a call from a good friend who was diagnosed with a serious, even life-threatening cancer. She was devastated. She vacillated between depression and hysteria. She had battled cancer in the past, and had won, but she was convinced that this was more than she could take.

She called me because she thought I was some expert, someone who could give her a way out, an answer. But she reminded me that, when it comes to suffering, there is NO suffering, like MY suffering! Job is lurking right beneath the surface of all of our lives.

Of course, we have moments when we know we don't have it so bad. But give us an opportunity for illness, addictions, emotional problems and dysfunction, and we will latch onto it. It is part of our communal weakness, part of our humanity. We can all wallow in misery. We are mired in victim-ness. We teach it to our kids! Have you noticed how kids are not responsible for anything? And we are all prone to that. If it is not illness unto death, it is how I am a victim of unfairness, intolerance, distrust, disrespect. You name it. We can bore one another into a coma about how unfair life is. And when you are waxing eloquent about your problems, your sickness, your bad luck, I can't wait for you to shut up so I can bore you with my story. It is so bad that if we meet someone who is chronically happy, we think it must be a condition we should medicate. If we are not totally miserable, we simply live lives that are pointless, unfocused and without passion.

What happens when life slams us with reality? We become individuals who are content to merely MAINTAIN our own existence. Even people of faith become content to merely MANAGE their relationship with God. But life is not meant to be merely "maintained." Our relationship with God is not something to be merely "managed."

The Job in us represents the human condition without Jesus.

31

Now, here comes Mark's Gospel. Mark, the oldest and shortest Gospel may be constantly focused on the CROSS. But…but it gives constant glimpses of the Resurrection and Pascal Mystery too. Mark helps us to see that the healing ministry of Jesus is closely bound up with his own suffering and death.

Job gets depressed. Mark gets real. There is a difference. Mark gives us Christ in a wide range of human experiences: in the Synagogue, in human intimacy, among friends and community and family. Jesus gets involved with his disciples and their in-laws! Jesus becomes a walking relationship with real people. Jesus can be found in the marketplace and in the quiet place. He is never far from his people. He is never far from healing, forgiving and raising up. But he is also never far from his own suffering.

It is no accident that from the ground of the real world, from the experience of sickness, pain, sorrow, sin and death, Jesus proclaims the GOOD NEWS!

Jesus transforms private lives, family gatherings, social situations and secluded moments.

If only Job had known Christ. What about you and me? What Job didn't know from the get-go we simply have to remember: in our lives, in our human relationships and in our solitude, WE ARE NOT LIMITED TO SICKNESS, BROKENNESS AND PAIN. Our devastating diagnoses, our dysfunctional families…all these and more…are places where we can meet the Christ.

One spiritual writer has said that the call of the wounded and the sick is not an empty cry in an endless night but rather an invitation from God himself to enter into intimacy beyond our imagining. The shudders and quaking of a fractured world, the seemingly hopeless economy, the war and greed…these need not be a prelude to destruction. Rather, they are a challenge from a co-creating God who calls us to so much more.

We are not Job. We are Jesus. And we have something exciting and liberating and hopeful to say about pain, sickness and trouble. We are different. And I say this to all those who would say, "You don't have to be a believer to survive in this world."

And to those who would say, "I don't have to go to Mass to be a good person," I say this: Life is not about "surviving" or being "good." Life is about soaring transformation and being GREAT.

At this Eucharist—and this is why Sunday Eucharist is so essential—at this Eucharist and at every Eucharist, we can look at the Job in all of us and know that, with Jesus, there is something MORE for us…so much more.

I am going to make a confession that may confirm in many minds, my strangeness: I am not a big fan of the circus. I wasn't even as a child. Clowns on unicycles juggling balls were boring. Lions jumping through blazing hoops were unimpressive. And three rings of activity all at once don't hold my interest.

That being said, one thing that did always impress me and still does is the ability of one trapeze artist to leave the security of his or her swinging bar and have enough trust that another person swinging up there would indeed grasp him. That takes a lot of courage and trust.

This week is Ash Wednesday and Lent begins. I think this image of the trapeze artist is a good one for Lent, at least it is for me. And today's readings are a great introduction and confirmation of that.

How much trust did Isaiah need to leave behind the security of his own images of a mighty God and trust that his unworthiness would be burned away so that he could say, "Here I am, send me"?

How much trust did Paul have to have to leave behind his intellectually secure attitude of persecuting Christians and trust God's grace to move him into a totally different life?

And let's talk about the disciples in the Gospel. They had worked all night. They were content to call it a day and wash their nets. They were following the conventional wisdom of avoiding the "deep water." Don't we do the same? But like the trapeze artist they had to have the courage to trust this passing preacher and start all over.

And face it, in a sense, the haul of fish could have been as impressive as a lion jumping through a blazing hoop. The haul of fish could have been explained away as a fluke or a passing school. But after that, they had the courage to leave everything about their secure lives and follow Jesus. That's impressive.

Lent will be our call, our opportunity to risk the deep water, to risk our nets in the unknown, to risk flying off our bar and finally to follow Jesus into change and transformation.

Risking the deep water is risking our emotional security and trusting that we are capable of something different and even great. It is putting aside our discouragement and exhaustion and trying again.

Risking our nets is letting go of earthly comfort. (That's the fasting part, by the way.) It is imagining that our old nets won't break and can hold so much more.

Risking our future is the commitment to follow Jesus. There will always be those who think we are crazy. You know, the ones with no imagination, the ones who have already returned to shore, the ones filled with doubt and discouragement. Don't let them determine your leap of faith.

God and Faith give us what we need to let go. Let go of our doubts so as to believe. Let go of our need to control life and give it to God. Let go of our sins and guilt and grab on to God's mercy, especially this year. Let go of feelings of unworthiness and let God purify us. Let go of anything that holds us back. Lent is time for flying off that secure bar knowing God will grab hold of you.

Sixth Sunday in Ordinary Time (B)
Mark 1:40-45

On Wednesday night we began our year of studying scripture in our All Ages Catholic Teaching (AACT) sessions. Of course, we began with some basic things that we need to learn about the Bible and God's revelation. Today's Gospel is a prime example of how one cannot simply read the Bible and presume to claim understanding. There is always more.

Leprosy, for example, in Mark's Gospel, is not about a terrible skin disease. It is about alienation and exclusion. It symbolizes SIN. And we don't know whether Jesus told the guy not to tell anyone. We do know that Mark uses the idea of the messianic secret to drive home the fact that, while the idea of a Messiah is something that should not be spread prematurely, nevertheless it is so exciting it cannot be hidden.

If we read this Gospel passage and picture a peaceful, serene pastoral scene with Jesus gently passing out a healing, we have missed the boat. This event was packed with emotion. The guy was desperate, daring Jesus to touch him, heal him, let him return to his family and his life. Jesus was not "moved with pity" as our translation says but, as the Greek verbs indicate, shaken to the entrails. And the healing wasn't about giving some guy baby soft skin. Rather it is the proclamation of the power of the Cross to cleanse our sin and restore us to our place in the community.

In touching the man, Jesus became the outcast, according to Jewish law. He didn't slip off to some quiet place just to be alone and pray. The law banished him. But the people, not Jesus, repudiate that broken-down old law and seek him out anyway because they know he is offering a new insight, a new law, a new lease on life.

But then we move on to the important part of the Bible and Gospels. Mark offers US an antidote to the superficial, saccharine Christianity that we have become comfortable with—the old holy-card-and-catechism Jesus who has nothing to do with the real thing.

Mark issues a radical manifesto of discipleship. This healing is an act of social subversion for Jesus. Without saying a word, he challenges the religion of the leaders who would stigmatize people for their illnesses. And when Jesus sends the man off to the priest, it is an "in your face" kind of action. The man is really going to the priest to say, "Nah, nah, nah. You said no one should touch me. But Jesus touched me. To hell with your superficial, selfish, man-made laws."

Mark's Gospel is terse and unpolished. Mark's Gospel is about work. We need to get the leper off the page and into our heart, with all his sores and dirt and isolation. We need to get Jesus out of the words and into our blood and figure out what the gospel means for us today.

You know, I have never seen a leper with boils and pus, standing on the edge of my life. But I have seen someone with AIDS whose family refused to visit, let alone touch. I have seen people with mental illness struggle to be accepted and respected. I know people who make racist decisions about where they'll live, where their kids will go to school and where they'll eat dinner—all the while pretending to be followers of Christ. I have had the marriage of a young man whose parents spent the whole reception apologizing to their social circle because their son married outside the parameters of their respectability. Who is the unclean one in such cases?

The lepers may be those who stand in front of us in the grocery store who know we judge them unclean or untouchable. They know we don't want them standing next to us. They know we don't want to see them sleeping under our bridges. When we pray for the homeless, sometimes the unspoken prayer is that they will just disappear.

We are surrounded by lepers of many kinds. We need to ask the question, "How will we address them?"

But more often than not, if leprosy is seen as a symbol for sin, WE are the leper. So, the bigger question is, can we acknowledge the unclean places in ourselves? Those sins are like an open sore in our souls. Dare we touch the place and seek a healing?

You see, in today's Gospel, Mark helps us see that much of what passes as Christian faith is vapid and shallow, if not distorted. Oh yes, we "go to" Church…so we don't have to take it to where we live! We learn about our religion and then promptly compartmentalize it, so it won't interfere with our prejudices and mental leprosy.

But Jesus was about something else. Discipleship is about something else. There is an incredible and exuberant joy at being healed and made whole and restored to the community. It is a joy we can receive and also give. But it begins with an honest humbling request, that Jesus would die to hear, if you catch my drift. He would die—he did die—to hear us say, "Lord, I need to be made clean."

Seventh Sunday in Ordinary Time (A)
Matthew 5:38-48

What Jesus hits us with today is so baffling, we either must ignore it or pretend we never heard it, or, when that fails, turn it inside out and discuss it into oblivion.

We look for revenge in certain cases. We want capital punishment in specific incidences. We need to create enemies so we can maintain our status quo socially, politically, nationally, and even spiritually. We don't want the gospel to play hardball with us. We want to feel GOOD about our relationship with Jesus. We don't want demands put on our rationalization and our narrow-mindedness.

The Jesuit writer and preacher James Kavanaugh tells of the time when he gave a lecture on "Capital Punishment and Disarmament in Light of the Gospels." Even after his well-crafted, rational, biblically based presentation he had to admit defeat when a voice from the back of the lecture hall said, "How can you be against war and capital punishment? Even Christ said, 'an eye for an eye, and a tooth for a tooth.'"

Kavanaugh acknowledges that it would have done no good to quote the rest of Jesus' statement and point out the man's stupidity. People hear what they want to hear so they can continue to think and believe and do what they wish.

The fact is, everything in our being recoils from the words of Jesus. We want more than an eye for an eye! Who really expects me to give up my coat? Love enemies? Don't be absurd. We work hard at creating enemies. We have trouble loving some family members let alone the Taliban.

Our individual resistance to the gospel is reflected even in our Church which has often been an institution meting out death rather than a faith community sustained by love.

My personal rejection of what Jesus says is reflected in the home and the church where I try to isolate myself…in the politicians I elect who support my prejudices…in the government I support even as we wage wars, oppress the poor and ignore the most vulnerable in our own land.

39

Depending on your personal religious bias, you can reject the gospel and still claim to be a spiritual person. Depending on your personal political bias you can, by turns, lay the blame on Bush or Obama or Congress or the Republicans or the Democrats. But the fact is, our resistance to the gospel is all of a piece. To hold myself not accountable is to hold my nation or church or family not accountable. My refusal to change allows me to accept the fact that the world won't change.

This is a hard gospel message and no amount of scriptural gerrymandering will provide us with valid excuses.

Plainly stated, the way of Jesus stands in stark contrast to our personal wars as well as our public wars. The way of Jesus stands in clear judgment of our hatred, our racism, our warmongering, our desire for revenge.

It is not easy. And none of us is innocent. The demons of this world and the demons in our hearts seduce us into thinking that the ways of Jesus cannot be followed in this time-bound earthly journey of ours. It is not easy. A woman gets gunned down a few blocks away…A young man gets shot on the other side of town…A young woman is kidnapped and trafficked into white slavery…A child is sexually assaulted by a member of her own family. There is so much that rears its ugly head and provides us with excuses to ignore Jesus.

And yet. And yet. In spite of our weakness and sinfulness, in the midst of our violence and murder, in the face of our fear and anger, our God says plainly:

"Take no revenge."
"The Spirit of God dwells in you."
"Love your enemies."
"Be perfect as your Father is perfect."

What will we do with that? If our God can say all that to us, it must be possible. If Jesus died for us, it must be possible for us to live for one another. If our God has so much faith in us, in spite of our sinfulness, who are we not to have more faith in ourselves, more faith in one another and more faith in what is possible?

Easter, Pentecost, Holy Trinity, Corpus Christi—all those celebrations are behind us now, and today we are plunged back into Ordinary Time. And the Gospel is the conclusion of the Sermon on the Mount. The temptation of preachers and readers of Scripture is to take passages out of context. By doing that, people might get to push their own agenda, but they often miss the big picture.

So, before we consider today's Gospel, let's do a quick review of the Sermon on the Mount. First, there were the beatitudes in which Jesus sketches the attitudes needed to enter the kingdom. (Poverty, hunger and thirst for justice, compassion, mercy, integrity, peacemaking and willingness to die for the gospel.)

Next, he gives the images of salt and light, emphasizing how important we are to the transformation of the world. He challenges his followers to a righteousness that outstrips that of the Pharisees, and he shows us how to go beyond the words to the root of the commandments about murder and anger and adultery and love of neighbor.

Next, he instructs us to carry out the three great acts of Old Testament piety: prayer, fasting and almsgiving. And he offers advice from Jewish wisdom.

He concludes with warnings to enter through the narrow gate and today's passage, about it not being enough to simply say, "Lord, Lord" or even to prophesy. Rather, today we learn that we must ACT upon ALL the things Jesus has taught.

The Sermon on the Mount is, of course, a stirring piece of rhetoric. Public speakers and politicians could learn a lot from Jesus' style. It is also a great treatise on ethics. Mostly it is a PRACTICAL DOCUMENT showing ordinary people how to live. The whole Sermon on the Mount, not just today's conclusion, is the rock on which we must build our house.

Rabbi Harold Kushner tells the story of a prominent rabbi who ran into a member of his congregation on the street. The rabbi said: "I haven't seen you at temple the past few weeks. Is everything alright?"

The man answered, "everything is fine, but I've been worshipping at a small synagogue across town." "I'm really surprised to hear that," the rabbi responded. "I know the rabbi of that congregation. He's a nice enough fellow, but he is not the scholar I am. What can you possibly get from leaving my synagogue to worship at his?"

The congregant replied, "That's all very true Rabbi, but he has other qualities. For example, he can read minds, and he's teaching us to read minds. I'll show you. Think of something. I'll read your mind." The rabbi concentrated for a few moments; the congregant then ventured, "You were thinking of the verse from Psalm 16 which says, 'I have set the Lord before me at all times…I have set the Lord before me at all times.'"

The rabbi laughed, "You couldn't be more wrong. I wasn't thinking about that at all. It was the furthest thing from my mind." The congregant shrugged, "I know you weren't thinking that. That's why I don't worship at your synagogue anymore."

There you have it. But don't excuse yourselves because the clergyman was the butt of that little story. Anyone of us can be guilty of not having the Lord before us at all times. Anyone of us can turn our Christianity into mere words and creeds, scripture quoting and attending the "right church" with all the prestige or power or even good preaching but with no real lived faith. If you are looking for a church, the consideration shouldn't be

—whether the people like me;
—whether I feel good there;
—whether the preaching is inspirational;
—whether it is prestigious…

Rather you should be asking

—Is this a diverse microcosm of the universal church?
—Am I uncomfortable enough to make necessary changes in my life?
—Does the preaching challenge me to move outside myself?
—Are the poor and the marginalized made to feel welcome?
—Would Jesus want to be here?

Today Jesus makes it clear that faith is not lived merely in buildings bearing God's name or in organizations espousing the right causes. Faith is grounded in values of the heart, everyday acts of charity, generosity, justice, and true worship that leads to action. Like we learned last Sunday, true faith is what leads to Eucharist and flows from Eucharist.

Today Jesus exhorts US to put his words into action. He challenges US to bridge the chasm between what we say we believe and what guides our decisions. Faithful discipleship is not about mere intelligence or even sincerity. It is about really putting the love of God before us always, as the center of our lives, so we may respond with conviction and integrity.

LENT & EASTER SEASON

And so, we begin our Lenten desert retreat with Jesus. Traditionally, we mark this time with acts of sacrifice. And all that is fine and good—as long as you don't use those things to AVOID the REAL CHALLENGE of Lent! And that is precisely a deeper relationship with Jesus…QUIET TIME WITH JESUS…time to look to that silent place within you where the Spirit lives.

Listen to today's Gospel…and all the Gospels. Sometimes, as good spiritual writers so clearly point out, the Church/the institution and we ourselves are very clever about replacing real gospel demands with our petty penances and rules. As though giving up chocolate or alcohol is on a par with healing broken relationships or giving to the poor.

No, the Gospel does not ask so much that we give stuff up as much as it invites us into a relationship. That's the radical message.

Haven't you ever thought it odd that after we read the Gospel that says clearly wash your face and stop being hypocrites, we go immediately and smear ashes on our face and parade around like we have fulfilled some obligation or accomplished something great???

I am here to tell you that if you "just came for ashes," you have missed the point. The ashes are the beginning ritual. They are not the main event. Don't be part of this world where style trumps substance and appearance commands more attention than honesty and integrity. Lent invites us to wash the ashes off, embrace a soul-deep conversion, find an inner peace, and walk with Jesus.

The scene painted by the first reading from Genesis and the scene painted in the Gospel of Matthew seem very different, but the connection is important. In Genesis we read:

"The Lord God planted a garden in Eden. And, out of the ground the Lord God made various trees grow that were delightful to look at and good for food. It was in the lush garden that Adam and Eve succumbed to temptation."

But in the Gospel, we see that Jesus was in no Garden of Eden. He was led by the Spirit into the desert to be tempted by the devil. It was in the harshness of the desert that Jesus was able to resist temptation.

Maybe lush gardens and arid deserts are not so different after all. It is what's inside us that matters. It is what we WILL that transforms us.

In the publication *The Christian Century,* Fred Bahnson wrote an article "Acacias in the Desert." He tells about the Sahel, the 3,000-mile stretch dividing the Sahara Desert and Africa's tropical forests. Over the years, the Sahel became more and more of a desert itself. Water is precious. The dry earth bakes at temperatures reaching 120 degrees. Meager crops can hardly ward off the famine that invariably grips the region. Life is precarious for the poor farmers who struggle to survive there.

But ecologists seem to have found a way for the Sahel to bloom once again. It's the acacia tree. The trees were once plentiful in the region until farmers began to cut them to increase the available land to cultivate. They yielded to the temptation to replace the trees with more open land they thought would provide food and income. But they were misled. The acacia tree stores water and nitrogen; its leaves produce mulch; its seeds are high in protein. Agricultural and relief organizations are helping farmers in the Sahel to replant rows of acacia trees on their land, then planting their crops between the rows. The trees act as a living fence protecting the plantings from the dry desert winds and preventing erosion.

Over the past 20 years, villages have seen their crop production double and triple. The land is healing. The people have rediscovered the wisdom of an old African proverb, "The one who cares for trees will not go hungry."

I believe all this speaks clearly to us about our Lenten experience. Each year we begin Lent in the desert. With Jesus we embrace the opportunity to lay our hearts bare and be vulnerable. We will be tempted, there is no doubt. But we can transform the desert of Lent into the garden of Easter.

This Lent borrow the symbol of the acacia tree. Move beyond empty fasting and trivial practices. Do something different.

In the desert of this Lent, in your life, in your heart, plant trees that store the water of compassion. Cultivate trees that grow the leaves of justice; trees that yield the seeds of peace; trees that can heal the broken earth of our hearts.

To be sure, there are harsh winds that blow through our lives; there are famines of despair that wilt our resolve and tsunamis that erupt in the human heart; there are the many fears that wear down our spirits. And there is the desert of Lent, at once foreboding and promising. If we go into the desert of Lent with Jesus and plant the right trees in our lives, we can realize a harvest of fulfillment and hope.

Planting trees in the desert of Lent will enable us to walk with Jesus into the Springtime of Easter where those trees of grateful prayer and unselfish charity will continue to bloom and grow.

This (past) week, I had a house guest here at St. Luke. John Norton was in town from St. Paul, Minnesota to meet with ACTION pastors and lead us through some dialogue about institutional racism and the spiritual and social change that is necessary. He arrived Wednesday night and came to Ash Wednesday Mass. Some of you may recall that I talked about how "repent" actually means "to change your mind."

Thursday night, I was working on my homily for today and John walked into my office and said that he hoped I would continue to develop that notion of change.

On Friday, John went out in the parking lot to jog. He collapsed and died. It was a stunning and tragic event for all of us. But John's words convinced me that we must continue to think about the basic Lenten call to "change our minds." And so, I offer this reflection.

Mallory McDuff is a mom and a college professor who writes for the *Huffington Post*. She seems to have made the connection between the Lenten call to change and some of the old-fashioned Lenten observances that many people have written off. She says:

"As a Christian, I give up something for Lent because Jesus went into the wilderness to fast for forty days and I want to share that. Jesus' battle with the devil was not just a personal fight but a battle for the soul of humanity. I want to be part of that.

"As a mother, I give up something for Lent because I want my daughters to know that I can survive six weeks without drinking a beer after work, and they don't have to be slaves to their own consumption.

"As a teacher, I give up something for Lent because I am weary of checking emails and Facebook and internet headlines and I need a break, a pause, to let Jesus find me and to find out who I really am.

"As a child of God, I give up something for Lent because I have experienced the loss of my mother and father and an unborn child and a marriage that crashed and burned, and I need to know that I am more than my losses.

"As a person of hope, I give up something for Lent because I want to prepare for a celebration. I need to open myself to the full celebration of Easter."

When you consider what she says, it is obvious that all that giving up isn't just some detached Lenten penance on a checklist. It is about changing the person she is into the person she wants to be.

All that fasting is more than self-denial; it is about refocusing on what and who is important in her life.

All that self-denial is about making time and space to "turn around," which is what conversion means.

A Lent without sacrifice and self-denial is a Lent without change. And a Lent without change simply leaves us in our cynicism, our self-absorption, our anger and our despair. A Lent without change is nothing more than checking days off the calendar.

Whatever you fast from—food, drink, media, shopping, an over-scheduled calendar, harsh words, impatience, your need to be in control—whatever you fast from, it can change you. And the "changed you" can withstand any temptation, any devil, any disappointment.

Benedictine Sister Joan Chittister says, "Lent is not about penance. Lent is the grace to change what we ought to have changed but have not."

John Martens writes, "And the word Abraham first heard from God, the command to sacrifice his beloved son, Isaac, remains even now at some level inconceivable and incomprehensible."

Abraham could not have liked what he heard. He was indeed a man of faith, but he was also a man of feeling, a man with a miraculously born son he was now asked to sacrifice.

Yes, WE know it was a test. Remember, Abraham didn't. So what did Abraham do? He prepared to follow God's word. BUT HE ALSO KEPT ON LISTENING.

How often does it happen to us? We hear God's Word, but it is not the word we want. We discover God's will, but it is not our will.

—God speaks and someone in our life becomes a disappointment, a worry, a devastation, even a loss.

—God speaks and an event crashes in on us that is overwhelming, hopeless, even tragic.

—God speaks and our first thought is, "I can't do this. God can't mean this."

Like Abraham, we need to keep on listening. God is never finished. God always has more to say to us.

We have been brought up to think of God as unchanging, absolute, detached. But that is not the God that Jesus reveals to us. It is not even the God of the Old Testament as we have mistakenly misinterpreted. If Lent teaches us anything, it is that, with God, even death is not a final Word. And I might add that even Resurrection is not the final Word. We haven't even begun to think about what God's next word might be. But it is the nature of God that he is never finished speaking a creative word to us. Never. Not even after we die. Not even after we "get to heaven" as it were.

Do you really think that if you get to heaven, God is finished speaking to you? It is only the beginning!

The voice that Abraham heard both times was true. It was true beyond factual. True because it revealed, both times, the depth of God's relationship with him and with us. If Abraham had only listened the one time, God would never have been revealed.

The same thing happens in the Gospel, of course. Jesus, always in quiet conversation with his Father, somehow heard the word of suffering, the word of Calvary. But he trusted and kept on listening.

The apostles stood in the midst of glory, terrified, and heard the voice of God, "This is my Beloved, listen to him." Obviously, the God who spoke to them in a vision of heavenly glory also was speaking to them when Jesus said he would suffer and die. Seemingly different messages. But when you listen to God, you don't get to pick just the "good stuff" according to your own judgment.

When you get to that quiet place with Jesus where the Father speaks to you, you will discover a place you want to return to over and over, knowing God always has more in store.

Third Sunday of Lent (A)
John 4:5-42

Today's Gospel was very long and so my reflections today will be a little briefer. Remember, there is power in the Word proclaimed even before anyone talks about it.

Water was obviously central to today's scriptures. So, for a moment, think about water in your life. We start out human life in the watery womb. We begin our life in Christ in the waters of Baptism. Our life is sustained by water. We drink it. We bathe in it. We need it to water the earth. Plants live by water. Even in the desert, water is needed to sustain those plants we think of as never needing water. Once a year, very briefly, the desert blooms with incredible beauty because water brings seeds quickly to life.

A great sage, renowned for his wisdom, told his students that water was his greatest teacher. He explained that water is unyielding but at the same time, all conquering. Water extinguishes fire, but when overcome by flames it turns into steam and re-forms as water. Water can wash away soft earth and moves easily around unyielding rock. Water saturates iron into rusted dust. It saturates the atmosphere and eliminates wind. Water is gentle, yet all powerful. He concluded by saying all students must make themselves like water, acting from a place of stillness and overcoming the world.

In the first reading the Israelites complained about the lack of water. They were so thirsty that their life of slavery in Egypt began to look good to them. And God gives them living water FROM A ROCK!

The setting of the Gospel is the village well. The well was the center of life in any village. It was where the women gathered each morning to carry water for all their daily use. But it was also the place where they caught up on the town gossip, received and gave support to one another. It was the place where the children played. The men would come to the well to water their flocks and to refresh themselves.

But obviously the woman in today's Gospel avoided the busy times at the well. She was probably the object of gossip by the town women, and the men would avoid her in public because she had a bad reputation. She comes at an off time, a quiet time, with her empty vessel to get her water and leave quickly.

But Jesus had another plan. Her empty vessel is an important symbol. All of us come to Jesus as an empty vessel that only he can fill.

Of course, we try all our lives to fill ourselves up with other water, but only the water that Jesus gives will really quench our thirst, cleanse us, fill us up and refresh us. We too come with our empty vessel. Did you think this Gospel was just about some woman in Samaria, a bit of interesting bible history? Of course not.

It is about us, in our Lenten desert, finding Jesus in the quiet place we have reserved for ourselves. Do you remember that I suggested that, when you go to your quiet place, don't bring anything? No music, no bottle of water, that ubiquitous appendage that has become part of the American anatomy. You must go to Jesus with the awareness that you are an empty vessel. And here comes the best part:

"The woman left her water jar and went into the town and said to the people, 'Come see a man who told me everything I have done. Could he possibly be the Messiah?'"

All that talk about water, and she never fills up her jar at the well. That is significant. Jesus transported her beyond the need for physical fulfillment and earthly water. He filled her with living water. Without anger or rancor, he prods the woman to face the reality of her life, the messes she has made of her relationships, the sin that has estranged her from her own people. Without raising his voice in condemnation, he brings her to an awareness of what she must do.

Now she is filled with living water. She doesn't even need the jar anymore. She becomes a disciple. She becomes an evangelist before the word was even created.

Jesus is inviting us to leave our emptiness here…Face our sins and shortcomings. He is gently inviting us to first be reconciled and then, like the woman, go to our people, whoever they are, and tell them what the Messiah has done for you. As much as we might like to, we can't hang around the well all day talking with Jesus.

There is work to be done, and no one is exempt.

We all must be reconciled.

We all must carry the word to our families and friends, to all those back in the village.

Last week it was the metaphor of thirst—and the woman receiving life giving water at the well. Today it is the metaphor of blindness—and the man plunging into faith at the pool of Siloam. Baptismal imagery abounds in these magnificent gospel accounts of quenched thirst, vision and spiritual insight.

The woman at the well gradually came to an awareness of who Jesus was. And she arrived at full faith, so much so that she became a disciple, preaching to others about Jesus. The blind man becomes more and more able to see with his heart. He also moves from recognizing Jesus as a prophet, then seeing him as the Son of Man and finally worshipping him as Lord. The blind man too is a disciple, preaching to the close-minded leaders about Jesus.

Last week it was the unheard-of situation of a woman and a Samaritan becoming an instrument of God's grace. Today it is about the unlikely leadership of a blind man living on the fringes of society.

Jesus too was an unconventional leader in the eyes of both the blind man's neighbors and the other leaders. In today's Gospel, everyone objects to his actions.

The man's neighbors debate about the man's identity, insisting they do not see what they see. When the healed man settles his identity for them, they shift to questioning how the healing took place. They further resist the explanation of the man who can now see. Like a bunch of contemporary politicians, they turn everything good into something bad, so they don't need to embrace anything outside their narrow agenda, which is the rejection of Jesus.

Finally, the neighbors, still unwilling to embrace faith, turn it over to their so-called leaders who continue the resistance.

The Pharisees question how the cure came to be. Next, they move to calling Jesus a sinner because he did the healing on the Sabbath. When the blind man acclaims Jesus as a prophet, the so-called leaders absurdly revert to questioning whether the man had been blind at all. They refuse to recognize the works of God being made visible. And they think they can see.

It is all so clear to us when we look at THEM! THEIR blindness is obvious. Of course, we think we can see just fine. But we don't. This Gospel is a wake-up call for us. Our blindness abounds.

We live in families that are riddled with alcoholism, unbridled selfishness and alienation, and we close our eyes to it all hoping it will go away.

We find ourselves in a Church that plays with words while it ignores the need for deep and lasting spiritual renewal. It dabbles in candlelight and ignores radical hospitality. It reduces the Body of Christ to a devotion rather than a sacrament of vibrant transformation. And we embrace the blindness.

We live in communities that are overrun with violence, where 14-year-olds have automatic weapons, where drugs abound in our high schools, and we blindly delude ourselves into thinking that there is nothing we can do.

We barely survive in a country that puts criminals to death, takes the life of the unborn, oppresses the poor, wages unjust wars, supports corporate greed and is in political shambles, all the while convincing ourselves there is nothing we can do.

We subsist on a planet that is being rapidly destroyed. There is global power mongering. There is our insatiable gluttony for unsustainable energy. There is the plundering of our very eco-systems. Yet we keep asking empty questions like Pharisees who choose to be blind to the answers that are right before us.

Who is blind, indeed? Who is thirsty? These Lenten Gospels are clear. Go to the well…but know you can never just go home again with your little bottle of water. You must be willing to become a disciple who will speak truth to power and who will bring others to Christ.

Go to the pool of Siloam…but know that when the mud is washed from your eyes, you must take a stand for Christ no matter who or what is throwing up obstacles. We can choose thirst and blindness. Or we can choose life and light.

The world of the elder brother. We are all in it. The fact is, there are more elder brothers than prodigals among us. Elder brothers don't need to be elder or even a brother. The "elder brother" syndrome could be the attitude of a younger sister or anyone else. You may be one yourself. It is the elder brothers who make the world work for all of us. They follow the rules. They cover for the slip-ups. They keep things running for their loving fathers and mothers.

We get where the elder brother is coming from. His resentment is our own. The elder brother is angry. We know he shouldn't be, but he is. And we understand that anger.

But the elder brother has a sin too. It is a lack of trust. The "elder brother" syndrome is one of constant anxiety. When prodigals are being prodigals, before they begin the road home, they don't stay awake at night fretting about what they have done or not done.

The elder brother is constantly anxious and increasingly resentful—that he may not be able to fix things, that the life he works so hard for will come apart, that he will let his father down, that no one appreciates what he does, that his loyalty and obedience are being taken for granted.

One of the favorite lines of the elder brother, even today is, "…after all I've done for you."

This isn't really the parable of the prodigal son only. It is the parable of two brothers…or two sisters…or two of any of us. It is a parable of God's forgiveness, which is always unearned and undeserved.

Face it, we don't know that the prodigal son was really sorry. Oh, he had rehearsed his lines. But maybe he was just tired or hungry and realized which side his bread was buttered on. The father ran out to embrace and forgive him even before he said he was sorry because that's what forgiveness is.

True forgiveness doesn't wait for an apology, or even that change of heart we have been talking about. In fact, for prodigals, maybe the change of heart comes AFTER the forgiveness. For all of us.

And we don't know that the elder son was so perfect. Obviously, he wasn't because no one is. But the father loved him all along anyway.

But think back on what the father did for each one. He embraced the prodigal, gave him back his dignity, restored him to the family. To the elder son he said, probably with his hand on his heart, "you are always here with me..." What better place to be but "in the father?"

Yes, this is a parable for each of us, for any two of us, for all of us. Oh, you can stay away from home and lick your wounds and feel sorry for yourself. You can absent yourself from the party and be hard-hearted and resentful. Or you can come on home, come on in. The father has already forgiven you, already embraced you. What are you waiting for?

Fifth Sunday of Lent (B)
John 12:20-33

Last Sunday over 100 of us gathered for our AACT session. We recalled some of the stories, true stories, of bombed out and burned out churches where statues of Jesus were found in the rubble. In these cases, the hands and/or feet of the statue were destroyed beyond recognition. Rather than recasting or buying new statues, it was decided to repair the statues without their hands and feet. One of these actually hung in the seminary where I began my formation. Along with all these repaired images, there was a sign that read simply: "You are the hands and feet of Christ."

Then, in age appropriate groups, we went on to discuss some of the problems and issues in our families, in our world, in politics, in our Church. Then individuals said how they would fix things if they were the hands and feet of Christ. We gave image to the whole session by tracing and cutting our own hands and feet and attaching them to a bare cross. Kids and adults understood it very well. That session, like today's Gospel, was about discipleship:

"Whoever serves me must follow me."
"Unless the grain of wheat falls to the ground and dies, it remains a grain of wheat."
"Sir, we would like to see Jesus."

So many in our world, including us here, want desperately to see Jesus. How can that happen, except through the laying down of our lives in service to one another? Some of our fellow travelers, our coworkers, our fellow students, our friends, might come to see Jesus a bit more clearly in each one of us. It doesn't end with Jesus.

During Holy Week we sing a song. We sing, "And he laid down, and he laid down, he laid down his life for you and me." It is more than a sentimental recalling of what Jesus did. It is us following, becoming the seed, dying with Jesus so others can see him.

59

Very recently, Sister Helen Prejean spoke at St. Charles. Most of us know her from the movie *Dead Man Walking*. Matthew Poncelet, the convict on death row, tells Sister Helen that he is not afraid of dying. He says, "Me and God, we got things all squared away. I know Jesus died on the cross for us. And he's gonna be there when I appear before God on judgment day."

Sister Helen responds, "Matt, redemption isn't some kind of free admission ticket that you get because Jesus paid the price. You've got to participate. You've got some work to do."

Sister Helen draws that thin line between the heresy that says we can earn or merit salvation by doing thus and so on one hand, and the reality that proclaims salvation as a free gift to those who embrace Jesus' invitation to be his hands and feet, on the other hand. In other words, to live and die as he did in service to others.

If all I do is recall how Jesus died for me and feel smug, I may as well be on death row. But Jesus has so much more in mind for us…And for all the people who say to us in so many different ways, "We would like to see Jesus."

"Unless the grain of wheat falls to the ground and dies, it remains just a grain of wheat."

Indeed.

In the Gospel just read, Mark makes a point that the donkey was borrowed. I think it is significant. Jesus enters Jerusalem, seated on a borrowed donkey, acclaimed by the lowly crowds as the one who comes in the name of the Lord.

What kind of Messiah makes his grand entrance on a borrowed donkey in front of a bunch of common people? You can bet there were no temple leaders or people of power out there waving branches. But that "borrowedness" is the unbroken thread in the story of Jesus. He was born in a borrowed place and laid in a borrowed manger. As he travelled, he had no possessions or place to lay his head, so he spent his nights in a borrowed space somewhere. He ate his final meal in a borrowed room. And when he died, his body was placed in a borrowed tomb. Don't you see a pattern here?

Jesus owns nothing, he possesses nothing, he takes nothing for himself. We could say his only possessions are compassion, love and forgiveness, and he gives those away without limit.

Such poverty is what he asks of those who would follow him. It is what Pope Francis keeps reminding us that the Church should be. Such poverty is the treasure of the kingdom of God—a kingdom built of justice, of mercy, of reconciliation, of peace.

And yet we who follow Jesus have so much by comparison. We want to acquire so much; we strive for so much. We measure status by possessions, houses, cars, who controls the check book, who has the key ring. We latch on to so called evangelists who preach a gospel of prosperity instead of the Gospel of Jesus where the poor are always first.

It is Palm Sunday again. We get another opportunity to follow Jesus into another Holy Week, to join him in emptying himself. Maybe this time we will get it. We follow a Messiah who possesses nothing but who has it all and is willing to give it all away. Let us follow him then, with a lively faith.

There are probably more people in this Church today than there were at the Crucifixion. Most people would have stayed away for fear of an uprising. There would have probably been the ambulance chasers of the day. The ones that went to every execution out of morbid curiosity. Maybe a couple of religious leaders were there just to make sure Jesus died. A few soldiers who were assigned the duty.

John's Passion makes it clear that Jesus disciples were not present for whatever reasons. Mary, the mother of Jesus was there. And her sister Mary the wife of Clopas. Mary Magdalene. And John, the beloved disciple.

They stood there and watched as Jesus died, much like we might gather at the deathbed of someone we love. They probably assisted with the hasty burial. They walked from the garden tomb together, bewildered, sad, supporting one another.

Think for a moment of the thoughts racing through their heads. What would your thoughts have been if you were there? What are your thoughts today, since you are here? Think about it. Reflect on it.

The mother Mary. From the moment of his birth, she knew something would happen. Even if she wasn't sure what. Mothers know. She watched him grow and move in a direction she knew would bring rejection. Now, though devastated, she trusted that somehow God would right her son's unjust and horrible death. A mother's love never fails.

The other Mary. We don't know much about her. John makes it clear that in her own grief, she stands with her sister. Of all of them, she might have been most aware that this was a dangerous place for them to be. Anything could happen. But this is her family, her kin. In them she has known the love of God. It never occurs to her to be someplace else.

Mary Magdalene. We don't know for sure what happened to her. We do know she was healed of a serious affliction or illness by Jesus. From then on, she led the company of women who followed the Teacher and tended to his needs. This Jesus gave her life, hope and a purpose that she refused to surrender, even when all seemed lost. She wouldn't give up now.

John, the beloved disciple. Maybe he wanted to run away like the others. No doubt he was frightened too. But he and Jesus had a special connection. There was a pull and a power that lashed him to that cross in a way he couldn't fully understand himself. He had to be there. For Jesus, for Mary, for himself. He sensed that even in death, Jesus would remain present to him. A disciple's spirit never loses hope.

And what about us? Here we are, with the three Marys, with the beloved disciple, with one another. Each with our own thoughts. Each with our own fears. Each with our own hopes. Where else would we be? Why are we here? Think about it. Reflect on it.

At the end of the Passion reading today, Jesus says, "It is finished." Most of us have been there in one way or another. All of us will be there at some point. And it is not just about death. Father James Martin, in a meditation on Good Friday, points out that we have all seen things come to a sad end, seen a project fail. You know, when you pour your heart and soul into something you planned for, saved for, hoped for. It is devastating when our hopes are dashed.

Maybe you didn't get the job you wanted. Maybe you lost the job you had. Maybe you lost your home. You may have had your dreams for a lasting marriage dashed. Or maybe your desire to get married was never fulfilled. You may have had dreams for your children that never materialized. Maybe you've lost the health you once had.

When such things and worse happen, it is normal to feel, with infinite sadness, "it's over" or "it is finished."

Today, Jesus is with us on this. When he hung on that cross, abandoned and in pain, he probably had many questions. What would happen to his disciples, to his mother after he died? Would they continue to live as he did and put his word into practice? Would the miracles they had witnessed sustain them? There is the experience of physical pain and spiritual pain, of course. But there is also the pain of lost possibilities.

But we have Easter. We cannot go through the agony of Good Friday without remembering Easter Sunday.

Jesus may have felt that the disciples would never gather again, that his teachings would be forgotten, but the Father had other plans. And we, in spite of our weaknesses, are witnesses to that.

As he hung on the cross, Jesus may not have been able to see how his work would continue. But the Father did. God can use everything we bring him, even our dashed hopes.

And so, in our own Good Fridays, when we feel that our dreams are ending, God has other dreams. We may feel that things have not worked out, but God has other workings in mind. We may think that hope is dead, but God is the source of all hope.

The 14th century mystic, Blessed Julian of Norwich said, "All shall be well, all shall be well, and all manner of things shall be well." A more contemporary expression goes, "everything will be ok in the end. And if it's not ok, then it's not the end."

On Good Friday, we focus on suffering, loss and death. But Good Friday is not the end.

In all four Gospel accounts of the Resurrection, Mary of Magdala, alone or with other women, first discovers that Jesus' tomb has been opened and the body she or they have come to prepare for burial is missing. The women run to tell the other disciples, becoming the first to proclaim the Good News! The rest of the details differ from one Gospel to another: in some, Simon Peter and the other male disciples must run to see for themselves before they believe; exactly when the women and the men first know and share the news varies; and in each, the encounters with angels and even the Risen Christ happen at different points in the narrative.*

Mark's Gospel, the oldest Gospel, ends on a very disappointing note. So, it is likely a sadly truthful note. Mark says:

"They ran away from the tomb frightened out of their wits.
They said nothing to anyone, for they were afraid."

Christians have been running from the Resurrection ever since. Really. Even though we might claim otherwise. (We are afraid of the "new life" we don't know.)

This sad fact reminded me of a line from an old country-western song from the late 60s. There may be no one here who remembers Bobbie Gentry. In her 70s now, she doesn't perform anymore, and probably wouldn't look good in those red toreador pants and high heeled boots anyway. But I had to dig out a very old vinyl record to make sure I had remembered it correctly. In a song called "Casket Vignette," she wrote, "Everyone wants to get to heaven, Miss Morgan, but nobody wants to die."

How true that is. Like so many things in life, we divide and compartmentalize. We can't handle the fullness of mystery, so we cut it up and miss the point. Yes, Christians run from Resurrection. But that running is more than fear of death. At a deeper, unconscious level it is the human temptation to run from the divine Presence.

Some are so afraid of the divine presence, they deny it. They call themselves atheists. But many so called Christians are "practical atheists." They claim and verbalize belief in God, but they run from God—they run from their true identity.

That's because, God and our true identity—our True Self—make demands on us. That oft quoted contemplative writer Richard Rohr says that our False Self fools us into thinking we are not, at our deepest level, spiritual. And we say it all the time. "Oh, I'm only human." That is a lie! We are NOT only human! It is an excuse we use to let ourselves off the hook when we know we are called to something greater. It is how we run from Resurrection and the divine presence on a daily basis, all the while, claiming to be followers of Jesus.

Our False Self distracts us with petty preoccupations, so we miss the radical reality. As I reminded you on Good Friday, Jesus held on to the pain, but he did not hold on to the Resurrection. He released it on the world. Resurrection is more than a gift or something that happens to us. Resurrection is who we really are.

Yes, resurrection is who we really are, but I speak from experience when I say it is hard to remember that when life is happening to you. You all have witnessed and prayed me through some great difficulty the past few months. It was hard not to share that pain. (And sometimes I did.)

One friend who has had treatments and recurring cancer for the last 20 years said it so well. She said, "Even when I am having a good day, I don't want to tell anyone. I am afraid they will stop praying for me. I am afraid they will think I am well. I am afraid they will leave me alone with my pain." She may not realize that her survival—her resurrections for 20 years—is what she really needs to share.

But it is hard. So, we run from our own resurrection and dwell on to the pain of life as we know it.

That is the False Self that drives all of us in one way or another…the False Self that runs from resurrection because of what lies between.

67

It seems that none of us is ready for the hard contact with reality that Jesus offers in his Incarnation: his Passion…Death…and Resurrection. We just want to make it all pretty. But it is much more important than all that.

Which is the illusion, death or Resurrection? Jesus showed us we don't need to even ask the question.

It is still true. Everybody wants to go to heaven, but nobody wants to die. Jesus died once and for all of us. That is the hard-to-grasp Paschal Mystery. That's what Christians foolishly run from— the Paschal Mystery. It is true that life entails many things. Life can throw a lot at us. But ultimately, life is about one thing: RESURRECTION.

[*Note: The author's original notes for this homily said only to "acknowledge the four Evangelists' accounts of the Resurrection," so descriptions the author used elsewhere were used to create the opening paragraph.]

In his book, *The Liberators*, Michael Hirsch tells the stories, impressions and reactions of American soldiers who liberated the Nazi concentration camps as they chased the last remnants of the Nazi army at the end of World War II.

He also includes the recollection of one of those liberated. Conrad Rood was a 24-year-old Dutch Jew who was arrested in 1942 and spent three years imprisoned in Nazi camps. In 1945 he lay dying in a covered ditch in a camp when the 14th Armored Division liberated the camp.

Rood remembers that he heard his friend speaking English and saying to someone, "Go in there, my friend is dying. He should know that he is free before he dies." Then he recalls that the trapdoor over the ditch opened up and there was an American soldier who said to him: "Come friend, you are free now." Rood recalls that he was crawling on the ground trying to get to the trap door and crying. Then the soldier picked him up by the collar of his little jacket and grabbed hold of him and pulled him out. All Rood could think of was how strong that soldier was. Then the soldier repeated: "You're free now. You understand? It's over."

Rood says, "As dirty and sick as I was, that American soldier kissed me and took me outside into the light and said, "See, you really are free now." And the soldier cried too.

After the liberation, Rood was reunited with his wife who survived the war in hiding. They made a new life for themselves in the United States.

The words of the American soldier were, "YOU ARE FREE; IT'S OVER." The words of the angel at the tomb were: "WHY DO YOU SEEK THE LIVING AMONG THE DEAD?" Ultimately, the message is the same.

Easter is God's never-ending invitation to freedom, his raising us up from the tombs of selfishness and fear and anger and hatred. In the many manifestations of his compassion and mercy around us, God picks us up and carries us out of our prisons and ditches.

And then, and then, we in turn become liberators ourselves, picking up others from among the dead, leaving behind our own fears and anger, restoring others to life and hope. That's the thing about resurrection and new life. It can't end with you.

In the light of Easter's empty tomb, every moment of forgiveness and every triumph of justice proclaims that Jesus is risen. Every rejection of vengeance and every instance of goodness (especially in the face of evil) proclaims that we are all free. Every act of compassion and mercy proclaims the good news that all are called to new life.

And with Christ Risen, you are indeed free.

We are called to be conspirators. In our parlance, "conspirator" or "conspiracy" has only a negative connotation, because we usually apply it to people who conspire to do bad things. But at its root, the Latin is "con-spirito" and means "with one spirit" or "with one breath."

Barbara Reid, a writer for *America* magazine says this about today's Gospel: "In today's Gospel, the risen Christ reinfuses the breath of life into the constricted lungs of the believing community, releasing them from the fear that choked their ability to ***breathe together*** and live fully for his mission."

So, Jesus calls his followers to a conspiratorial faith, conspiring to do the right thing, breathing to do the right thing. But before he can do that he must break through their locked doors, overcome their fear, give them peace and get them to accept reality.

"Peace be with you" are his first words to them. Then what does he do? He shows them his hands and his side.

"Peace be with you. Look what they did to me."

"Peace be with you. The bad stuff really happened."

It's not like he walked in and someone said, "Hey Jesus, how you doin?" And he said, "Fine, good, everything's great."

How trivial that would have been. His Passion was intimately bound up with his Resurrection. You can't have one without the other. Of course, if we tried that, no one would come near us:

"Peace be with you. I've lost my job."

"Peace be with you. I am worried about my daughter and her relationship with her abusive boyfriend."

"Peace be with you. Things are not going well at home."

"Peace be with you. I'm flunking English."

"Peace be with you. I am worried about some tests at the hospital."

In our culture it is considered bad form to admit weaknesses. We trivialize everything. We put on a show. And so we never "conspire." We never breathe together. We never truly heal.

71

On that first Easter night, Jesus refused to pretend that nothing had happened. True peace—and true faith—are possible only when we deal seriously with the hurts we endure and the wounds we inflict on others. Only when we face it and deal with it can there be peace, forgiveness and healing. Then we can take a deep breath together and conspire to be disciples of Jesus.

Peace and healing do not happen in an instant. True peace recognizes the horror of what has occurred and results from a willingness to enter into a PROCESS of healing and forgiveness.

Moreover, our peace, our healing, our ability to breathe together comes only when, like Thomas, we open ourselves to reality and pursue a personal encounter with Christ.

Our breathing together is not a second-hand faith. Other believers and even unlikely events can lead us to Jesus, but then we need an experience of Christ. Jesus says, "Peace be with you." His peace rests on each of us. Then we take a deep breath together. We conspire to become the **Body** of Christ.

The road to Emmaus often represents the road of despair or disappointment or sadness or even anger. It is a road that all of us walk in various times of our lives. One message of this Gospel is that this road is where Jesus walks with us, even if unseen. Another message of the Gospel is that this is also the road of hope, in spite of our apparent feelings. A third message is that the experience of the Emmaus road must be shared.

Rebecca Bateson tells the story of her six-year-old son Andrew who came down with bacterial meningitis. In order to save his life, the doctors had to amputate both legs where the disease had destroyed his circulatory system. Of course, Andrew and his family were devastated. Rebecca couldn't handle it. She wondered how a six-year-old could. Then one night, after months and months of agonizing rehab and prosthetic legs, Andrew said offhandedly. "I saw God, Mommy, when I was sleeping in the hospital. He put his arms out and I thought he was going to hug me. But instead he touched me on the shoulder." Rebecca steeled herself and asked, "Did God say anything?" "No, he was just…there," Andrew said, and he went on eating his supper.

That's the story of the Road to Emmaus. The Risen Christ is just…there. Maybe in our aloneness, maybe in the presence of family or friends or doctors or nurses or teachers. Maybe in a spouse or a co-worker. He is just there.

An interesting aside and I think purposeful: The Gospel never says who the other disciple was. It just mentions Cleopas. In our chauvinism, we just assume it was another male disciple. We even picture it that way in art. But the Gospel doesn't tell us. And there were women in Jesus' company too. They were the first ones to discover the Resurrection. Maybe the other disciple was Cleopas' wife. Or his teenage son. Maybe in their disappointment and sadness, she said to her husband, "Let's get out of here. It's not safe in Jerusalem. Let's go over to Emmaus for the day. We'll have lunch and come back." The point is, Jesus walks with us whether we see him or not.

That second message is about how the followers of Jesus move from wishing to being grounded in true hope. They were wishing that someone would rescue them from their situation. What they got was an entirely new story, a new way of seeing and hearts inflamed with hope.

When Václav Havel was elected president of the Czech Republic, he offered these words on hope: "Hope is a state of the mind, not of the world. Hope is a dimension of the soul...It is not the joy of things going well but rather the ability to work for something because it is good, not just because it has a chance to succeed. Hope is not the conviction that something will turn out well, but the certainty that something makes sense, regardless of how it turns out."

Luke is really saying the same thing in the Gospel. It is about how hope began to burn in the hearts of those first followers of Jesus. They were blindly fleeing from Jerusalem because things did not turn out according to their wishes, THEN, they come to see that Jesus' death is not an end. Nor is his Resurrection an isolated event. Rather it is all about a new way of life in a world that is changed.

The third message is that they also see they must live this new life Eucharistically...not in isolation or even in private rejoicing. Their hope is not a private thing. Their hope is fanned into a flame that enables them to live for others. The two in today's Gospel felt compelled to return to Jerusalem, the place where prophets were killed. They had to go back and share their news.

The Emmaus Road story is about how sight is transformed, hope is enkindled, and witnessing is clarified...Not in a single instant or in one magical moment, but in a lengthy process of praying, learning the Scriptures, walking with others, breaking the Bread and sharing our faith. The Emmaus Road is a lifetime journey. The Jesus we thought we knew vanishes. The Risen Christ, whom we don't always recognize, remains.

Most of the time, either by choice or by default, we live very small, compartmentalized and narrow spiritual lives. Through his Passion and Death and certainly in today's Gospel, Jesus is inviting us to live large, live fully. He doesn't invite us to do this in the way people usually mean when they say, "live large!" He invites us to do this in a way that embraces our full potential…that embraces not just the person of Jesus but the Risen Christ, the Cosmic Christ.

In light of today's Gospel, we do this in three ways: as DISCIPLES, as BELIEVERS and as WITNESSES.

First, disciples: We are not just lone rangers. We are a community of people. You don't encounter the Risen Christ as isolated individuals. That is not how the Resurrection works. The disciples were gathered together, for lots of reasons. Maybe they were frightened. Maybe they just needed to be together. But real disciples form a community. Maybe they did have doubts. Maybe they did think they were seeing a ghost. But at least they were together to check on their sanity. Jesus can be just as unreal to us sometimes. Even so-called Christians can be incredulous. And haven't we all found ourselves "wondering" at times? As disciples we encounter Christ in community. Disciples need to be a community of people.

Second, believers. As believers we are a Eucharistic people. That's what makes us different. We move from being disciples and a community of people to being believers and a Eucharistic community. It is more intimate. That's what Jesus was trying to help them see when he said, "Have you anything here to eat?" Our translation from the Greek is much too formal. It was more like, "What do you guys have to eat here?" It was like family coming home and raiding the refrigerator. It was real. It was intimate. Jesus was drawing them into a tighter circle than just a circle of disciples. They couldn't remain incredulous. He was there in front of them, wounds visible, eating a piece of fish.

Third, witnesses. Once Jesus bridges the gap between death and life...once disciples move from community to Communion...once we make the jump from incredulous to intimate, we are filled with hope, filled with the Spirit. We can't remain mere believers. We can't stop the progress. We can't limit the Resurrection.

It is always the same. At the tomb, Mary was sent forth to tell the others. To be a witness. At the end of the story on the Road to Emmaus, the disciples were sent back to tell the others they had seen Jesus in the breaking of the bread. In today's Gospel Jesus says, "You are witnesses..."

So, then, who is Jesus for us? Only a vague spiritual entity? Or is Jesus so real, so here and now, that our Sunday Eucharist is, indeed, an eating and drinking with Jesus, a "Mass to Mission" sending forth by Jesus to bear witness?

See how it works? We go from disciples to believers to witnesses. To do anything else is to limit the Resurrection and short circuit the Spirit.

Fourth Sunday of Easter (B)
John 10:11-18

Today, hopefully, many inspiring homilies will be heard throughout the Catholic world as preachers try to take this image of the Good Shepherd, which is already a favorite among believers, and help people comprehend the incredible love God has for his people. There will be stories about smelly sheep and wooly lambs, about wolves and predators, about pastoral practice in the middle east in the time of Jesus, hired hands vs. shepherds, about helpless, hapless sheep, about the dangers of shepherding in the Judean countryside, etc. etc. All of which may be helpful in getting contemporary Christians to plumb the depths of the fathomless love of God for his people.

And right now, as is often the case in the life of the flock of God, we need all the help we can get. We need all the reassurance and positive reinforcement we can muster.

—We've got personal issues and families on the skids.

—We've got more than the swine flu threatening our health and well-being.

—We've got social disasters and global disintegration.

—We've got economic fall-out that has people hungry, homeless and scared.

Everywhere we look we uncover more bad news. If we ever needed a Good Shepherd, it is now.

We might have preferred a private guide to navigate us away from or around all the disasters of life. But that is not what we are offered. We are offered a shepherd who loves us enough not to abandon us…Who walks with us through the perils that surround us…Who cares deeply enough to carry us, if necessary, right through the middle of all the bad stuff.

It is not a matter of sailing through life unscathed. It is a matter of surviving and growing through life rooted in faith that prompts us to answer the call to follow him.

Now here the homily could end, and we could all go home feeling a little better about our own personal Jesus being there for us.

77

But that's not going to happen. First of all, I have only been talking for a couple of minutes. Second, you know enough to realize that there is another critical component to this image of the Good Shepherd.

When Jesus rose on Easter, he did not rise as one guy who just continues to save his friends. No. When he rose from the dead, a community of believers was born, a shepherding community, a community that takes on every aspect of the work of the Good Shepherd. Will you get the shepherding you need? Count on it. Will you get saved from the big bad wolf and the edge of the cliff? It is part of the promise. But now it is intimately bound up with the shepherding you do for someone else.

This reminded me of Beverly Copper Butler. Our deacons have shared stories about her. There have been things in the bulletin. She is one of us, but because of her debilitating ALS, she has never been here. On the surface, she seems to be on the receiving end of ministry. To some people with no vision she may seem to live a worthless existence. But make no mistake about it: she is shepherding the Body of Christ in the parish as much as anyone.

Ironically enough, even in her physical state, or maybe because of it, Beverly is always looking for ways to give back, to reach out, to do something for others. Jesus is the Good Shepherd for her, and she has become the good shepherd for others.

And she is not alone. How many people in this parish face devastating odds, saddled with their own insurmountable problems, yet responsible for the shepherding of others…called to be Christ for someone else? We are surrounded by heroes: the wounded healers whose own illnesses enable them to reach out to others…the broken builders, whose own fractures give them power to put others together…the lonely lovers whose own solitude forms them into generous friends.

Even when their tempers grow short, their service remains long. In spite of their own pain, they manage to squeak out some comfort for others. Overcome with their own doubts, they still offer hope to someone else.

The Gospel began with Jesus saying, "I am the Good Shepherd." But you know, Jesus never just told us what to do, he showed us how to do it. And he expects us to follow through. This whole Gospel is put into the context of our Easter story, not someone else's.

Just look around. Then look no further. We have everything we need to do what needs to be done. We have everything we need to give what must be given.

We are the sheep. We are the Shepherd. We are the Body of Christ.

The image of the vine and the branches is a clear indication of how we are sustained by connections. Connection with Christ, of course. But the image Jesus uses is not only about connection to himself. If we are all branches of one true Vine, then it is also about our connection with one another. It is connection that saves and sustains us.

Maureen O'Rourke tells, in her story "In a Father's Final Days," how she was saved by a connection. When her father was dying of Alzheimer's she promised to be with him to the end. She was a career nurse and she was confident she could care for him. After pneumonia set in, death was imminent—or so she thought. He was taken to a nursing home, but she remained by his side, taking care of his physical needs as he slipped in and out of consciousness.

But her dad continued to hang on. She was determined to keep her promise. But after three weeks she was physically and emotionally exhausted. She remembers, "This one particular evening, I was thinking, this is it. I couldn't do it anymore. The next day was my birthday, and I was trying to figure out how to tell my dad, 'You know I love you. I'm sorry. I know I made this promise, but I just can't really keep at it.'"

Maureen continues, "Then the staff nurse came in to say goodnight to me and slipped me this little brown bag. In it was a small bottle of Bailey's Irish Cream. And she said to me, 'This is just for you. Maybe you could sip a little and be able to rest a bit tonight.' The gesture had nothing to do with being a nurse, it was just a human connection. She knew I was struggling, too, that it was difficult for me, and, the long and short of it is, I drank some Bailey's Irish Cream that night, I stayed with my dad, it was a long and difficult night, and my dad died at 7 in the morning."

"I don't think it was until after my dad died that it really struck me. Without that small gesture of kindness from that nurse, without that connection, I probably would have left that night, and my dad would have died alone."

You see, a simple kindness extended from one nurse to another, one daughter to another, mirrors Jesus' words that we are connected to one another, that we are branches of the same vine, a vine that is the source of nurture and support.

I would like to share another story, my own. As most of you know, I have been going through some difficult times and there are some days or weeks when I am not sure I can hang on. I know you know this because of the many cards and notes and gestures you have extended that remind me how important connections are.

Ironically, during this time, I have received several of those prayer shawls or small afghans that have become popular. I have a couple in my office and also in my room. When I take a nap, I use one. When I say my prayers, I put one on. When I just sit in my chair, one keeps me warm.

I was thinking, with compassion and care, skeins of yarn can be the vine of Christ to which we are all "grafted." I am reminded of the connections between Christ and us and between us and one another.

We are part of something greater than ourselves, something that transforms the fragility and the vulnerability of our lives, of my life.

Again, the image of the vine and the branches is not just comforting Bible talk. It is about a deep and abiding reality in our lives.

In our simplest acts of kindness, care and concern we live out Christ's image of the vine and the branches. No matter how frustrated we get, we are connected. No matter how cut-off we may feel, Christ continues to hold us to himself and join us to one another. No matter how alone we actually are, we celebrate our connection to one another in the Risen Christ.

About four weeks ago I had the opportunity to go to Pittsburgh and see the film *Of Gods and Men*. I was so touched and taken with the film that we are bringing it here next month for our monthly film night.

It is an extraordinary French film that recounts the true story of a small monastery of Trappist monks in a mountain village of Algeria in the 1990s. In the gruesome violence of the Algerian civil war, the community of eight monks was an oasis of peace and compassion in the midst of the horror around them.

The monks lived humbly, simply and happily among their Muslim neighbors. They kept their garden and bees. They offered hospitality in their guest house. They gave medical care to all who came to their small clinic. They did not try to convert any of their Muslim neighbors to Catholicism; yet their simple lives and generosity formed a bridge between Christianity and Islam.

As the violence escalated the government urged the monks to abandon the abbey and return the France. The monks anguished over what to do. Each monk had to decide.

A Muslim villager asked one of the monks if they were going to leave. The monk shrugged, "We're like birds on a branch. WE don't know if we'll leave." But a woman of the village pleaded, "No, we are the birds. You are the branch. If you go, we'll lose our footing."

In today's Gospel, Jesus assures his disciples he will not leave them orphaned. In the peace and blessing engendered in their simple lives, the Trappist monks became the "branch" of God's love and Christ's presence for both their Muslim and Christian neighbors.

Those monks were a sign of the Spirit of God speaking in all that is just and good, in every word of compassion, in the simplest acts of reconciliation and peace.

For whom could you be a branch?

The Spirit promised by Jesus "advocates" for what is good, right and just. This is true in spite of our skepticism, in spite of the rejection of the things of God in our world, in spite of the blindness that darkens our landscape. It is when things are bleakest that we need the Spirit. It is when we are most tossed and turned that our world needs a branch to hang onto.

We await Pentecost. We look for the Advocate to guide us in whatever opportunities we all have to be "branches" of hope and healing for those desperately seeking a place to alight. With the Spirit's indwelling we can be for one another, shelters welcoming the poor, the lost, the searching. There are people in your life searching for answers, struggling to find a way back, seeking a solid footing.

Jesus gave us the Spirit so that more than monks can be a safe haven and a place where the love of Christ prevails.

Luke tells us in Acts that, "In truth I see that God shows no partiality." Yet we grew up believing otherwise. Sometimes our Churches (Catholic and Protestant) preached otherwise. Often our parents taught us otherwise. In the so-called "good old days" God liked Catholics better than he liked Protestants. Today, God loves Christians better than he loves Muslims. Isn't that the attitude? And even when we are that stupid, God does not cut us off. We cut ourselves off. And let's not even get into the racial and ethnic convictions about God loving one more than the other. We still don't get it.

Yet, in spite of our messing it up over and over, Jesus can still say to us, "As the Father has loved me, so I also love you." And again, "It wasn't you who chose me, but I CHOSE you." Even having heard that we still don't get it.

The wonderful, universal embrace by God is narrowed down to God likes me or my kind or us the best. We actually reverse what we heard in the Letter of John.

We heard, "In this is love: not that we have loved God, but that God loved us." We think it is all about the fact that we love God…we follow the rules…we meet the criteria. We follow Jesus. And so we close those other people out of the circle. We still don't get it. It is really about God's initiative. In loving us, in choosing us, God give us a big responsibility.

Jesus came to show us the Father and we still don't get it. We quote Jesus and the Gospel and the Bible to justify our own exclusion of whoever we don't agree with.

Can't we begin to change our image of God? Can't we make some steps toward embracing God's love and mercy for ALL PEOPLE? Can't we become truly Catholic? Whatever our image of God is, it too often is NOT the image that Christ came to show us.

Suzanne Guthrie writes about her work as a hospital chaplain in a book called *Grace's Window*. Here is what she says:

"A hospital corridor can be a mysterious place, a terrible and holy threshold upon the boundary of the soul. Uprooted from your ordinary days, the hospital confounds the peaceful soul with the realization that the God of daily living is also the God of sudden dying. The God of the comfortable parish church is also the God of the intensive care unit. The God of candles and incense is the God of vomit and pus. The God of white linen altar cloth and embroidered chasuble is the God of plastic curtain and sweaty sheet. The God of pipe organ and flute is the God of squeaky gurney wheels and crying children. The God of altar wine and communion bread is the God of infected blood and wounded flesh."

Is that a little too graphic? Good. We need to be shaken loose from our preconceived notions about our neat and clean God because Jesus has transformed our relationship with him. Jesus touched lepers and embraced prostitutes. He associated with sinners of every stripe. He showed us that God indeed shows no partiality.

Still, in our private lives we persist in our arrogant exclusions of whoever is different. In our political lives we make decisions based on lying sound bites and narrow-minded judgment of people we don't even know. In our Church we condemn women religious who built the Church in this country, who dare to work with AIDS patients and minister to street people, who dare to live like Jesus in a frightened ecclesiastical culture of hypocrisy.

Indeed, deep down, we KNOW God is in places where we least expect. But we don't act like it. We KNOW God is present in all the terrifying places. But we don't live like it. We KNOW God is in all the messes of our complicated world. But that knowledge eludes us.

Today's message is at once comforting and more than challenging:

"God shows no partiality."

"As the Father has loved me, so I love you."

"I chose you."

85

Permanence or change? Permanence or change? We like the security of permanence. But we need the challenge of change. The Easter experience of the apostles reveals to us some things that bear witness to the tension between permanence and change.

On one hand, we know that God is ever the same…solid…a rock. Yet the Easter experience of the early Church and the first disciples was that God was an ever-renewed God. The resurrection of Jesus shattered the early church's expectations about God. In Jesus, something new had happened, something never-before imagined.

The first Christians saw themselves as faithful Jews, and, at the same time, something different. And they had the gift of the Holy Spirit to help them make sense out of their identity and their mission. The Holy Spirit is the wild card.

There is, as John Martens says, an inherent wildness in the Holy Spirit, a sort of un-tame-ability or un-manageable-ness. The work of the Holy Spirit challenges old ways of thinking and acting. The Holy Spirit at once brings peace and unsettles. The encounter of Peter and Cornelius shows this clearly. The new Church was, right off the bat, challenged to change. The Holy Spirit was given to Gentiles. How did that happen?! But it did, and the young Church had to deal with it. It had to broaden its understanding of itself.

When the Church continues to define itself by the past, as it usually does, it is always wrong. Right now, we have a Pope who, like Peter, is challenging us to rethink our identity, to reframe our mission. The Church needs to say "yes" to the Spirit and literally see what happens.

You cannot start seeing or understanding anything if you start with "no." "No" slaps labels on people and situations. "No" short circuits the Spirit. "No" excludes and marginalizes. But "yes" throws open the doors. "Yes" embraces and welcomes. "Yes" is the work of freedom and grace.

In my opinion, we are, as a Church in an unprecedented situation. We have the very top, the Holy Father. Then we have the very foundation, the folks in the pews and the marginalized and the poor. Both the top and the bottom, as it were, see clearly the need for a new Pentecost, a radical shift. Francis sees it. You all see it. You know something must change. Yet the whole middle management doesn't get it: bishops, bureaucrats and pastors. They are afraid of change, afraid of a loss of control, afraid of the Spirit.

The desire to hang on to the status quo is a clear indication that we have not been formed by the prophets or Jesus, that we have lost our prophetic voice. Jesus and the prophets criticized the institution, whether it was religion or politics, but always remained faithful to the real Tradition. Of course, they were also killed for it.

The insiders—the teachers, the Pharisees, the Roman leaders, the priests and the scribes—crucified Jesus. Think about it. Who are the insiders today? And they would crucify Jesus again, all the while proclaiming their own faithfulness to some gilded status quo or misguided tradition.

Do you know there are some bishops who won't allow the song "All Are Welcome" to be sung in their dioceses? Why? Because they are afraid some unworthy person will receive Communion. If you are ever in a Church where they begin the Communion Rite by announcing who can't receive Communion, run like the roof might cave in, because it might. And there are others who won't allow the song "Sing a New Church" to be sung. What are they afraid of? Who are they excluding? The Catholic Church, under the compassionate guidance of Francis, needs a groundswell.

So, what is this homily? Is it like a 1960s call to religious disobedience? Is it an invitation to march on the mansion of the Apostolic Delegate in Washington? Of course not.

But it is a declaration that, just as the Holy Spirit fell upon ALL who were listening to the Word, so that Spirit has been given to all of us. Be ready. It is a reminder that right before Jesus commanded us to love one another, he CHOSE us and appointed us to go and bear fruit. It is the proclamation that a new Pentecost is possible.

"The eleven." Not twelve. "They worshipped, but they doubted." The little community that re-assembled for a final meeting with the Risen Jesus was not the boastful Twelve. You remember, the ones who promised to die with Jesus…the ones who were feeling arrogant because they thought Jesus was going to restore the kingdom of Israel in some shallow political show of power. You remember those twelve!

Well here they are now, a broken "eleven." They are overwhelmed by loss, loss of Jesus, of course, but also loss of Judas, uncomfortably one of them. They are chastened by failure, ridden with guilt. Here they are. And instead of scolding them and telling them, "I told you so," and why didn't you listen, Jesus gives them the great commission. In this seemingly inept and fumbling group, Jesus sees promise and a future. And he tells them they will be his witnesses everywhere. He tells them to go and make disciples of all nations.

To us too, on this celebration of the Ascension, broken though we are by the vagaries of the world and our own sinfulness…sometimes doubting even as we worship…grieved by the absence of those who have been lost, like Judas…to us too Jesus gives the great commission. To us too is leveled the question, "Why do you stand here looking at the sky?" There are loved ones in your family who need attention. There is much brokenness in your community that needs to be fixed. There are young people in your life who need to be "eldered" by good example and love. There are the old and the weak among you who need to belong. Nothing good will happen if you just stand around looking holy, saying your prayers, feeling sorry for yourself and waiting for pie in the sky by and by.

And so today we get a big PUSH, but we get a big promise too. "I am with you always…"

Daniel is a 13-year-old boy. His family in Ethiopia was swept away by disease and conflict. He was adopted by a family in America. And although he flourished in many ways, he was always shrouded in feelings of fear and pessimism. He distrusted joy. The sound of laughter made him suspicious. Then came the junior high science fair. His mom wisely suggested that he do his project on the "science of happiness." He was skeptical but intrigued.

He discovered that happiness is not determined by wealth or status but by attitude. Happiness is found in relationships and experiences, he read. (But of course, we all know that, right?!) What made a powerful impact on Daniel was the idea that one cannot simply decide to be happier—one had to practice it. He read about an exercise called "the three blessings." It is scientifically proven that writing down, every day, three things that went well makes a person feel less depressed within three months.

His presentation was a big hit. His classmates loved it and he got an "A." Two years later, in ninth grade, he revisited the subject in more depth and earned another "A."

Daniel is now a junior and is thinking about college. He told his mom what he wanted to do: "I want to be the person who helps other people feel happy. Last year a boy from school committed suicide, you remember? He was sad because his girlfriend dumped him. I want to be the person who tells him, 'You can be happy.'" In his youthful enthusiasm, Daniel said, "That could be a job, right?" His mom assured him that being a psychologist or therapist is, indeed, a job. And Daniel said, "That's what I want to be."

Can't we all be that? A priest can certainly be that. And a teacher can be that. And a mother, a family member, a fellow worker can be that too. Maybe not professionally, or for money, but no less effectively. As Daniel seeks to be a means of the happiness he has discovered, so the Risen Christ calls the Eleven—and now us—to be the means for others to re-create their lives.

The Ascension isn't about Jesus leaving. It is about this great commission. We hear it all the time. Now we even have leadership that models it. Like Daniel, we can do this. What are we waiting for?

We always want to know what is going to happen next. I guess it is human nature. Most of the time, most of us have a hard time living in the moment. We spend too much time regretting the past or fretting over the future.

But we are in good company. Those first disciples were the same way. Think about it. As confusing as it was, they had experienced the Resurrection. They saw the Risen Christ on several occasions. They had the promise of the Spirit. You would think that would be enough to keep them happy for a long time.

Yet they were still bogged down with old expectations of the Messiah and unable to grasp the intensity of a new and different future. They were still hanging on to old comfortable notions. So they asked Jesus, "Lord, are you, at this time, going to restore the kingdom to Israel?"

But Jesus is very patient with them and simply reassured them of the coming of the Spirit. Then he commissioned them to be his witnesses.

It is the same with us. All we need to know is that we are to be witnesses to the life and Resurrection of Jesus. Not just some of us, not just the ones who can speak well, not just the perfect ones. All of us.

It is in being witnesses that our future unfolds. Whatever comes next for us must be discovered in the course of carrying out our mission. I guess you could say, if you don't carry out your mission, there is no need to worry about the future or what comes next, because you just don't have a future. And that is hell: not to have a future. Forget the image of being fried to a crisp in unquenchable fire.

It will not come as news…you all know it…we live in a very self-absorbed culture where self-proclaimed Christians have forgotten the cost of discipleship. Discipleship means being witnesses to Christ's presence in our broken and needy world.

The feast of the Ascension of Jesus is the smack in the head we all need to get over the wide-eyed wonder of Resurrection and get to work. Standing around waiting for the rapture is not an option. Only you can be the witness Christ needs in your time and place.

—The poor need you to be a witness, not just offer encouraging words.

—Your friends need you to be a witness, not just commiserate with them.

—Your children need you to be a witness, not support their self-absorption.

—Your family needs you to be a witness, not sacrifice your values to keep the peace.

—The Church needs you to be a witness, not simply shore up some old order that has not worked.

—The world needs you to be a witness to peace and justice.

Don't ask Jesus what comes next.
Be what comes next.
Be the disciple Christ has empowered you to be.

A few years back, I discovered I could speak in tongues. It happened again this week. One parishioner commented that he often nudges his wife during my homily because I am speaking to them. And many times, people will say it: "You were speaking directly to me last Sunday."

Don't get me wrong. I am not minimizing the gift of what is called *glossolalia*, that is, an ecstatic language. But I am talking about the very real and practical gift of the Spirit which enables each of you to hear just what you need, either in the Scripture readings or in the homily. It is about you and what you are disposed to. It is about the attitude, sometimes buried deep within you, that you bring into this Church.

All of those people we heard about in today's readings, they were Parthians, Medes and Elamites, and so on. They were from all over the known world. The Spirit brought them together and gave them what they needed. They heard what they needed to hear. They became believers. The Corinthians found out the same thing. They all had gifts from the Spirit and God used them to build up the Body of Christ on earth.

On this day of Pentecost, we celebrate the fact that the Spirit is still at work in the Church, even when we can't see it. We are still overflowing with gifts, even when things seem bleak.

Early last week I shared something with the daily Mass folks that is especially pertinent today as we celebrate who we are as a community of faith.

You know, we talk a lot about and have concern for the many people who are not here: our children and friends who no longer worship with us, the unchurched and non-believers who need to hear the Good News. We talk a lot about evangelization and sometimes mistakenly limit that to staving off the hemorrhage from the Church. And all of this is a worthy concern that needs our attention.

But today, on this feast of Pentecost, we need to celebrate what is still happening in the Church by the grace of the Holy Spirit. I want to share some statistics on how many people in the U.S. entered into the Catholic Church this past Easter.

The Galveston-Houston Diocese welcomed 2,300
The Archdiocese of Washington—1306
Atlanta—1,913
Los Angelas—1,666
New York—1,350
Newark—1,075
Seattle—1,045
Chicago—950
Youngstown—302

That is 10,005 from only nine Dioceses. There are 195 Dioceses in the country. Add to that 800,000 infant baptism this past year. Look at the record breaking crowds that swarm the Vatican every Wednesday to see and hear Pope Francis. There are no statistics for the United States, but it is reported that because of Francis, in Italy, the pews are filling up again because people are beginning to feel better about being Catholic. And we all know how hard it is to please those Italians.

Now we can say all we want about how great Francis is or what a good job some Diocese is doing with evangelization, or how effective a parish RCIA program is, or how good a particular homily might be…but the point is, it is all the work of the Spirit. It is what is in you and what is in me. It is because of the many gifts of the Spirit which are always unleashed in the Church even during times of drought and negativity. We have so much to celebrate.

And now, in conclusion, I am going to do something which is not my style and may even be a little hokey, but you will adjust. Peace be with you.

And now, just as we do before Communion, I ask you to congratulate one another on being part of something so much bigger than ourselves and offer one another the Peace of Christ.

Today is Pentecost. And I want to build an ark. Don't laugh. They laughed at Noah and look what happened to them. They got washed away in the deluge. I want to build an ark...and I want to build it with you. I want to build an ark, not because it is raining but because it is a way to preserve and offer what God has given us.

Let me explain. Last month I turned 70. Everyone wants to know if I am retiring. Not yet. (Sorry.) Of course, I would like to spend a little more time in Italy. And a little more time in the woods. But I am not retiring yet. I'd like to engage in some ark building first.

I recently read an article in *America* magazine that helped me clarify my dream for the future. It is important to have a future, right? I want US to build an ark. I think I have always wanted to do this. I think I have always tried to do this. But it is clearer now that I am older and wiser. I want St. Luke to be an ark with room on board for every living thing.

I realize we are living in a chaotic world and we are riding on waves of chaos. How do we navigate the chaos? In an ark. And remember, in the beginning, in the Book of Genesis, the Hebrew scriptures says the world was *tohuwabohu*, a watery abyss. Chaos. And out of that chaos, with the Spirit hovering above, God created the world. What does the Holy Spirit prayer say? "And we shall renew the face of the earth." It can happen again. From the Ark we can discover a renewed earth, just as Noah did.

In history the Church has been compared to a ship. Even the inside of a church building is called the "nave" from naval. But I like the ark image better.

In medieval times, great Cathedrals and sprawling Benedictine monasteries appeared on the landscape like ships...arks on the sea of the landscape. From those arks, they rebuilt the shattered economy. They re-establish the failed agriculture. They preserved intellectual heritage. They were a refuge of calm, hospitality and sanity for nearby villagers. From those arks they rode out the storms of the Dark Ages.

Can we build an ark that will be open for all who are having trouble navigating the waters of the 21st Century?

Can we build an ark that is open to all? What did the first reading say? We are Parthians, Medes, and Elamites, inhabitants of Mesopotamia, Judea and Cappadocia. Can we build an ark that is open to Christian, Muslim, Jew and even atheist? How else will they come to know our heart and know our God? We've got to stop yelling at them and calling them names. We must invite them into the ark.

Can we build an ark that is not shut up and closed, with no fear-battened hatches but with room for every living creature? That was Noah's secret. Can we build an ark that recognizes Christ in the gifts and needs of strangers and aliens? What did the Second reading say? "There are different kinds of gifts but the same spirit."

Do you trust that we can do it? It is Pentecost, give yourself some credit. We can do anything. Do you trust we can do it? (Can I get an amen?) I'm 70 years old. I have been a priest for 44 years this weekend. I know more than the pundits of politics and the pornographers of a corrupt culture and the hucksters of a blind religiosity…and so do you. This is something we can do. It is something I want to do until my body simply won't work anymore.

Can we build this ark? It is an ark from which we can send out a dove of peace to frightened old Roman hierarchs and liberal theologians. The disciples were frightened too. They locked themselves up. But the Spirit got through anyway.

Can we build this ark? It is an ark where American nuns and Girl Scouts and women who have been oppressed for centuries will be allowed to talk.

It is an ark where the old and the young can find a place, where the sick and the shipwrecked can find solace.

It is an ark that keeps sending out doves of Peace to the right and to the left, to the rich and to the poor, to the gifted and to the deprived until those doves return with olive branches that promise a future.

Can we build this ark?

ORDINARY TIME, PART 2

Robert Owens Scott writes in *Trinity News* of what he calls "A first memory of God."

"I was two or three," he remembers, "and I was angry about something. Very angry. I threw a tantrum and flew through the house crying and stomping. I ran and hid under my bed where I lay muttering to myself about how awful my mother was and how much she hated me. Finally, when I ran out of steam, I looked out from under the bed to see that my mother had been sitting quietly the whole time in the rocking chair, holding a glass of milk and patiently waiting. She wasn't angry at all, just waiting until I was ready to climb into her lap and be comforted."

He goes on to say, "This may be my earliest memory of any kind, a memory of God because it is what I think of when I read, GOD IS LOVE. This says so much more about God, about the Trinity, about how God relates to us, about how God loves us than any theologizing or philosophizing."

Today's solemnity of the Trinity celebrates the many ways that God makes his presence known in the manifestations of love in our lives and in our world. God is the very love that first creates us and then nurtures us and then preserves us. God is love that is father, mother, maker, son, sister, Spirit, friend.

Isn't the Spirit of God known in the loving grandmother, the patient neighbor, the many comforting, feminine presences that are woven into our lives?

Isn't the Son of God known in the strength of friends, the compassion of a stranger, the look in a hungry child's face, the gratitude in the eyes of the poor?

Isn't God the Father known in the firm hand of a mentor, the healing hand of a nurse, the guiding hand of our own fathers, the faithfulness of a pet, the beauty in all creation? Isn't God known in all of it?

The Trinity is best understood when it is taken out of the realm of faith and put into the reality of life.

The trinity is known in the Cosmic Christ that took the place of Jesus of Nazareth who came, in his own words, for only one purpose: to show us the Father.

The Trinity is best embraced when we look inside ourselves and uncover the ability to create, the willingness to save, the strength to keep breathing.

The Trinity is best celebrated when we stop living only for ourselves, when we commit to our own transformations as life demands, when we graduate from making small talk to making a difference.

God the Father, Son and Holy Spirit is the source of the forgiveness we give and receive and the reconciliation we work to bring about. The Trinity is not a formula...it is the justice we seek for every human being we call brother and sister.

God is the source of all good things. As we plunder our earth and selfishly consume our resources, the Spirit remains the air we breathe and the water that slakes our thirst and the regeneration of all that is possible.

God is the source of all good things. As we make war, kill our neighbor, turn our backs on one another, the Christ remains the peace that is always possible and the hope that we can achieve it.

God is the source of all good things. As we stomp our feet and throw our tantrums, God waits patiently in his big rocking chair with a glass of milk to calm us and a warm embrace that enfolds us in something much bigger than ourselves.

Today, together with Orthodox Christians, Eastern Rite Catholics, Anglicans, Lutherans and many other Protestant Christians, we Roman Catholics commemorate the martyrdom of Saints Peter and Paul. They were killed in Rome by the Emperor Nero around the year 67.

We recall today their faith, courage and leadership. But it is also a day to celebrate their differences and all the POSSIBILITIES.

Humanly speaking, the apostolic partnership of Peter and Paul should never have worked out. They had different backgrounds, different education, different personalities and temperaments. Yet, though different, they each received the call to discipleship.

There is that wonderful possibility that God take sinners and saints to enliven the Church with unity-in-diversity, with simplicity or scholarship, with service and witness, with silence and with worship.

For some reason, while writing these thoughts, this simple little song came marching out of my memory and I couldn't get it out.

"All God's creatures got a place in the choir.
Some sing low and some sing higher.
Some sing out loud on the telephone wire.
Some just clap their hands or paws or anything they got now."

(It distracted me. And after an hour watching YouTube videos of Celtic Thunder and the Clancy Brothers singing this song and more, I got back on task.)

For me, Peter and Paul are iconic of all the differences, all the contradictions and all the possibilities. No one—maybe especially the ones we marginalize—no one is immune from God's grace, God's call and a place in God's Church. No one. And the differences make for beauty.

There are excavations under St. Peter's Basilica in Rome, and they are one of the most interesting sites in the Eternal City. As you enter the long passageways under the basilica, you descend, down, down, through several layers of history until you come to a

99

necropolis, a city of the dead. You pass through narrow, damp passages to a small cavity where scratched on the stone in Latin are the words "Here is Peter." The general site was claimed as far back as the year 130 AD, but it was not until 1968 that there was any archeological proof. That crude, simple burial place is in sharp contrast to the magnificent basilica that now stands over it. Peter might be embarrassed. But Peter was a man of contrasts. We know his character was simple and impulsive. He speaks first and thinks later. The one who despite all his bravado ends up denying and deserting Christ, only to be named the Rock on which the Church is built. What is God doing?

Paul is not without his own contrasts, contradictions and possibilities. He was a zealous Pharisee who persecuted the Church and sought to silence the gospel. He presided over the stoning of Stephen. Then he became the most renowned preacher and spreader of the gospel message to places all over the then-known world. The once proud Pharisee wrote the very intimate and humble words of an old man in prison: "I have fought the good fight…I have run the race." The words remind us that the journey of faith is not a "walk in the park," but a "race in the stadium." No pain, no gain…no cross, no crown.

Both Peter and Paul ended up in prison. Both were martyred. Maybe the physical and emotional and spiritual prisons we find ourselves in, maybe the chains and narrow thoughts that bind us can be contradicted and turned into opportunities for growth and freedom.

From Peter to the murderous Borgia Popes, to John XXIII to Benedict to Francis—the Church survives or thrives. From Paul to St. Dominic to Hildegarde to Luther, to the inspired teachers and preachers of today, the gospel is preached and massaged and worked out. The gates of the kingdom, whose keys were given to St. Peter, have not been closed to anyone.

Jesus builds his Church on the Confession of St. Peter, on the preaching of St. Paul, on the work of many sinners and saints, on the faith of each one of you. The contradictions and differences are always there, and so the possibilities are endless. Everyone has a place in the choir.

Fourteenth Sunday in Ordinary Time (A)
Matthew 11:25-30

This past year, Nancy Kelton, a journalist for the *Boston Globe*, wrote an article entitled "The Students in the 'Do Nothing' Row." A brand-new substitute teacher was going in to temporarily replace the third-grade art teacher, Mrs. P., who was a long-time veteran. When the substitute walked into the classroom, she was struck by the arrangement of the students' desks. There were four vertical rows of four desks each. Then, along the back wall, in a horizontal row were five other desks. All 21 desks were occupied. She recalled what Mrs. P. had told her. She had said, "You can depend on the kids in the first four rows to do anything you ask. They will help pass out supplies, do their work, participate, whatever." She had gone on to warn, "Expect nothing from the one in the horizontal row. That's the 'do nothing' row. They come to school for lunch and recess and to use the lavatory."

As one boy in the "do nothing" row tapped his desk as if it were a drum, the substitute teacher introduced herself. She said she was not an art teacher and would love suggestions on how to use the time. The drummer pointed to a Dr. Seuss book the teacher had under her arm and asked her to read it. Another student wanted time to draw. She said they could do both. So, they all sat on the floor around the teacher and read the book together. Both the "do something" and the "do nothing" students read.

Then two "do somethings" and two "do nothings" passed out paper and crayons. The teacher said they could draw what they were reading about if they wanted. She told them they could keep their drawings or give them to her at the end of class. Everyone in the class read and drew and learned. At the end of the class most of the "do something" students and every single one of the "do nothings" handed in their drawings, looking for acceptance and recognition.

That teacher went on to become a full-time second grade teacher. She liked her students and they liked her. She became skilled at individualizing instruction and alternative ways to inspire children. There were never any "do nothing" rows in her classroom. That teacher is lifting burdens even today.

In today's Gospel, Jesus challenges us to see one another with the eyes of God...to behold the grace, the dignity, the potential that everyone possesses. Knowing about God is a gift given even to little ones and the most unexpected persons.

Just last week, in Rome, I visited, as I always do, the spectacular Piazza Navona, arguably one of the most beautiful squares in all of Europe. I was reminded of an experience I had a few years ago visiting the same piazza. And I have told this story many times. As my companions wandered around the Piazza looking at the sidewalk artists and the mimes, I focused on a disheveled, dirty street beggar, leaned up against a wall waiting for people to drop coins into his plastic dish. A few feet away at a small cafe table, sat a handsome and fashionably dressed Italian couple. As I watched, the couple got up, picked up espresso cups and walked over to the beggar. They said something to him, and he got up and followed them over toward the magnificent Bernini Fountain across the pedestrian street. Then all three of them sat on a step, she in her probably $600 shoes and designer dress, the man in his Armani suit, and the beggar in his rags. She offered the beggar her cup of coffee which he quickly accepted. I sidled over to eavesdrop on their conversation. I couldn't understand most of their exchange, but I know they talked about the Italian government and Berlusconi and an opera playing at the Caracalla Baths. There they were, this educated, fashionable couple who could have stepped from a magazine page, and this street beggar with seemingly nothing to offer. The couple threw no money into his plastic cup. But they gave him time, recognized his dignity and respected his knowledge. They lifted a burden that night.

Jesus invites all of us to know the Father: the bright and the not-so-bright; the learned; the big ones and the little ones.

Jesus invites all of us to come to him: the fashionable, the educated and even the ones from the "do nothing" row.

Jesus invites all of us to BE him: to lift burdens, to recognize dignity, and to erase the god-awful lines that society dupes us into drawing between one another.

102

Fourteenth Sunday in Ordinary Time (B)
Mark 6:1-6

In 1960, yet one more religious persecution broke out in the territory of Sudan. A Christian black student name Paride Taban fled the danger and went to Uganda. While in Uganda, he studied for the priesthood and was ordained. When things settled down in Sudan, young Fr. Taban returned to his homeland. He was assigned to a parish in Palotaka.

His African congregation found it hard to believe that he was really a priest. He says, "The people looked hard at me and asked, 'Do you mean to say, black man, that you are a priest? We can't believe it.'" They had never had a black priest before. They always had white priests who gave them food, clothing and medicine. Young Fr. Taban was from their tribe and had nothing to give them. He was poor like them. To make matters worse, Fr. Taban had to introduce them to the changes of the Second Vatican Council.

These changes were hard to accept. They said to one another, "This young black man turns our altar around and celebrates Mass in our own language. He cannot be a real priest."

So why did they find it hard to accept him? Was it because he was one of them? Was it because he was black like them? Was it because he didn't give them food or clothing? Was it because they did not want changes in the Church? I would suggest it was all of the above, and more for most people. Moreover, in spite of protests to the contrary, we are the same way. We want Jesus on our own terms.

In the Gospel today, Jesus was too much for them to deal with. And Jesus is often too much for us to deal with so we just short circuit his message, make it fundamental, strip it of dynamic power and make it manageable.

Jesus was and is always on the side of the crucified ones. Although every Christian Church claims him, he is not loyal just to one religion or this or that group. Jesus is wherever suffering is. He loves suffering Iraqis and suffering Americans. He loves Protestants and Catholics. He stands with the oppressed gay man and the oppressed married woman.

We do not like that. We want it cut and dried. We want Jesus to reflect our ideas. We want our own agenda. Jesus grabs our self-created boundaries away from us. We like boundaries because they make us feel secure and keep people out.

Moreover, Jesus showed us how to be comfortable with contradictions and even opposites. Yet we ignore him, creating divisions and reacting to differences, all the while claiming to be his followers.

Think about it. Jesus was human yet divine, heavenly yet earthly, physical yet spiritual, killed yet alive, powerless yet powerful, victim yet victor, failure yet redeemer, marginalized yet central, one man yet every person, in the flesh yet cosmic. Jesus had no trouble with contraries and contradictions. Could that be why the people of his hometown rejected him? Could it be why we reject him? Jesus said, "FOLLOW ME. BE LIKE ME." We twist it around. Instead of following him, we worship him. It is not the same. And we act differently than he did!

Yes, there is something in us that wants to reject Jesus. He is like us and we want him to be different. He is constantly introducing change and we want stability and sameness.

Of course, we are here because we believe in God's Word, the Tradition of the Church, the Real Presence of Christ in Eucharist. We believe in the personal encounter we have with Jesus in every sacrament.

And yet…and yet…

Today's Gospel challenges us to consider the many ways we reject Jesus. Don't focus on the people in the Gospel. Apply it to yourself. Jesus is more than we think, and he is all that we can be.

Sixteenth Sunday in Ordinary Time (A)
Matthew 13:24-43

Today's Gospel parable is loaded with imagery and points that are so pertinent:

—Pertinent for our individual spirituality.

—Pertinent for our Church as it strives under new leadership to be an image of Christ.

—Pertinent to our world as it faces unprecedented moral, political and economic devastation.

This Gospel passage addresses it all and it would take more than a few minutes to unpack it thoroughly. But we only have a few minutes.

Before I suggest some thoughts for your reflection, there is one, seemingly minor historical and biblical point that must be made. It is about the master, the good man, telling his servants to let the weeds grow with the wheat until harvest time.

Matthew uses the Greek word for weed, *zizania.* It is a specific weed. This weed looks a lot like wheat when it begins to grow, and it is not until late in the growing season that it can be distinguished. Keep that little detail in mind.

This parable introduces a householder who is gentle, patient, lenient and confident, not threatened. Interestingly, the theologian Walter Brueggemann gives us five adjectives for God: merciful, gracious, faithful, forgiving, and steadfast in love. Do you think maybe he got that from Jesus in the Gospels?!

However, the human ego wants a God we can comprehend. The human ego cannot comprehend all that mercy, all that faithfulness. And despite claims to the contrary, we really can't comprehend a God who is not judgmental. So, we make a God in our own image who reflects our culture, our biases, our economic, political and military systems. This is true for all people across the globe and for so-called Christians in America.

I am skeptical enough to think that it was not really faith that put "in God we Trust" on our money or "One nation under God" in our pledge of allegiance. It was our effort to have God protect what we think is important, even at the expense of others.

105

St. Augustine said, "If you can comprehend it, it is not God." Think about it. Would you really respect a God you could comprehend or control?

It is difficult to let God be greater than our projections. We want to have control. Instead of trying to "look like God" we want God to look like us. We want to tear out what we consider weeds, no matter what the cost. We want a God who plays at war, just like we do. We want a God who dominates, just like we do. We don't want a Lamb of God because we can't be that.

And yet, even we, with all our narrowness, are attracted to a gentler image. Like Pope Francis. Previous popes were more like us. Domineering, hell-bent on rules, ready to judge and pass judgment. Some of us complained about them. Some thought they were great. Yet, when one like Francis comes along, we are drawn in, in spite of ourselves.

But make no mistake about it. He is criticized by some who think he is too liberal and has not spoken out on several things, especially abortion, contraception and gay marriage, the firebrand banners behind which shallow Christians hide. However, Francis is clearly trying to set a new tone for the church, a tone that is more gospel oriented, a tone that will enable the Church to dialogue about such things, to speak to those who disagree with us about such things.

Francis said the Church should be a home for all. Does that sound a little like letting the weeds and wheat grow together? Of course the Church is opposed to abortion. Of course the Church is pro-life when it comes to birth control and capital punishment and war. Of course the Church upholds marriage as fundamental to our communal life.

But you don't save unborn babies by condemning abortionists and calling them names. You don't get couples to embrace a pro-life attitude by turning them away from the sacraments. You don't build up a culture that respects marriage by vilifying gay people.

Only God knows what is possible out in the fields. An evangelizing community does not grow judgmental or even impatient with what it considers weeds.

Where would we be if God were as judgmental and eager to rip things out as we are?

And right now, as we sit comfortably considering Scripture, we have people firing missiles at one another in a land that they both call "holy." Just because each sees the other as weeds. Yet both sides prayed for peace with Pope Francis just a few weeks ago.

Right now, as we sit here, a crisis unfolds in our own country. Its principal victims are impoverished children who so many consider weeds, with no right to grow in our fields.

The applications of this Gospel are infinite. Couldn't we start with ourselves and allow God to create us in the divine image? Not judgmental, not mean-spirited, not racist, not ready to slash and burn, not grudge-holding, not fickle, but merciful, patient, faithful, forgiving and steadfast in love.

Sixteenth Sunday in Ordinary Time (B)
Mark 6:30-34

In April of this year, the *Des Moines Register* carried a story that some of you may remember. Members of an Iowa synagogue awoke one morning to fine neo-Nazi graffiti covering the walls of their temple. The entire religious community, of all faiths, reacted with anger. Later, an eighteen-year-old boy and his seventeen-year-old girlfriend were arrested.

The community, still seething, demanded that the two be prosecuted to the full extent of the law—but first, the synagogue's rabbi wanted to talk with them. The two offenders met with the rabbi, two Holocaust survivors, a former member of the Israeli army and three temple elders. Fear, tears and anger flowed as the Jews told their stories of horror and Nazi atrocities and of struggles in a new homeland.

The teens told their stories and revealed so much pent-up anger and hurt. As a child, the young man had been physically abused and as a result had suffered significant hearing loss and a speech defect. He ran away at fifteen and was taken in by a white supremacist group. He was completely indoctrinated in bigotry and hate. He came to Iowa to start his own neo-Nazi group. His only recruit was the girl, herself convinced she was worthless and doomed to self-loathing.

The group met for hours. A dramatic change took place. The offended Jews saw two teens, lost, broken and frightened. The two young people began to see real people, not just stereotypes, people who, although hurt, were wise and strong.

It is not just a fairy-tale ending. In the Jewish tradition, forgiveness must be earned. The two performed 200 hours of service to the temple, 100 hours under the supervision of the custodian to restore the temple and 100 hours with the rabbi studying Jewish and Holocaust history. The temple got medical help for the young man and he had his Nazi tattoos removed. The two obtained job skills, therapy and their GEDs.

The atonement worked. The teens had their lives transformed. The community moved beyond anger and demands for blind justice.

In today's Gospel, Jesus calls US to seek out "deserted" places and quiet times so that we can bring restorative justice and reconciling peace to our families and communities too.

You don't need me to tell you how bombarded you are.

Advertising attacks, texting absurdity, voicemail invasions, social media madness, political diatribes, cultural violence, religious terrorism, even ecclesiastical threats.

Like Jesus and the disciples, we may find that the legitimate demands of people and our calendars and our responsibilities do not always cooperate. But we must persist in striving for that quiet time and place. We need time and space to hear the voice of God speaking in our hearts. We need to put aside our anger and fears, our egos and our need for control. Only then will we be people who accomplish, not just revenge or punishment, but restorative justice based on relationships, forgiveness and healing.

Lately, I have noticed that almost every venture into Scripture turns up for me an overwhelming awareness of the presence and the power of forgiveness and healing. And I ask myself if I am getting too narrow in my focus or is forgiveness and healing really at the root of every part of the gospel. I think I know the answer and so do you. Forgiveness and healing are what Jesus was all about. Forgiveness and healing come only to people who have responded to God's call to come away to a quiet place.

Seventeenth Sunday in Ordinary Time (A)
Matthew 13:44-52

What are you searching for? What do you do when you find it? Are you searching at all?

A teenager lost a contact lens while playing basketball in the driveway. After a brief, fruitless search, he gave up. But his mother went out and within minutes found the lens.

"How did you do that?" he asked. "We weren't looking for the same thing," she explained. "You were looking for a small piece of plastic. I was looking for $300."

The search for the gospel treasure and the pearl begins first with knowing what you lack and second, knowing the real value of what we are searching for. Then you need to invest the time and energy required.

In the first reading, Solomon understood what was needed to be truly great. The culture does not support such searching and such wisdom. It is a truism to say that most of us spend our whole lifetime searching for the wrong thing and, in fact, usually become impatient with the search, impatient with life really.

Moreover, if we paid more attention to life, we might find that we already have what we are searching for. We just haven't taken time to see it and embrace it.

An art history student studying in London was given an unusual assignment. She was to spend two hours in the National Gallery looking at a single, specific painting.

The two hours studying the subtleties of color and mood and composition was an experience she could not capture on paper or on Instagram or Twitter. It happened just as the professor knew it would. It filled her with mystery, wonder, surprise and otherness. These emotions are seldom felt in our "always connected, 24/7 digital culture." We shy away from introspection and reflection all the while considering ourselves very connected, very in touch and very important.

But again, that is what our culture does to us. When I vacation, I always take some pictures. I take them mostly for myself. After having the experience, it is always nice for me to look back, remember and relive it. And I don't usually bore people with vacation photos. If they ask to see them, fine. Remember how we all used to groan when someone would force us to watch home movies or slides of their latest trip?

People don't take time to reflect on, absorb or appreciate the moment. In days gone by, there were always those who lived their whole vacation through a camera lens. Now it is worse. They are constantly Instagramming, tweeting and emailing pictures of their experiences to people who can't really appreciate the moment and often don't care. Even with the best camera or phone you cannot capture the depth of feeling, experience, color or mood. That is what the young art student discovered.

It does not occur to us that sitting quietly in a magnificent basilica or on the edge of a breathtaking mountain range could change us. Taking a picture is not enough. When we take time to absorb it, we can bring to those we love more than a one-dimensional snapshot that never conveys what that moment did for us. We become a fuller person, a happier person, a person spiritually, not just digitally connected.

What we are searching for is often right in front of us, but our superficiality or lack of focus keep it hidden.

So, what are you searching for? What can you really share with the world? The wisdom, the treasure, the pearl of great price…they are all present, sometimes within and sometimes out there. Don't be so anxious to rip through the net, don't be so quick to discount what appears to be worthless. And don't miss the moment. Give it time. Don't give up the search. Let life wash over you. Don't presume your best days are behind you. Age, health, opportunity notwithstanding, there is always the possibility of greater days of discovery ahead. Let every experience make you wise. Don't travel through life so superficially that you miss it. Don't race past the pearl of great price.

111

I doubt that anyone actually counted the number on that grassy hillside. Certainly, it was a huge crowd. But who were they? In her book, *The Sacred Meal,* Nora Gallagher challenges us to consider who made up that group.

The sick certainly had come, hoping Jesus really was a wonder worker and they would be healed.

There had to be some exhausted moms with their kids in tow.

Unemployed workers were definitely there and also struggling farmers whose lives seemed hopeless.

Among those present, there must have been more than one who was dealing with a shattered relationship, a serious illness, or some other loss.

What about the depressed and homeless and disabled? They must have found a patch of grass to sit on that day.

Jesus' close friends had to be there, following him, along with some wealthy landowners.

On the edges of the crowd were probably those who were embarrassed to be there, who didn't want to be noticed: tax collectors, prostitutes, thieves, alcoholics, addicts. Jesus seemed to attract that group in spite of themselves.

And don't forget some of Jesus' harshest critics: Pharisees, scribes, priests. They had to be there keeping an eye on this rabble rouser, Jesus.

Yes, they all found a place on the grass: the happy and the troubled, the doubting and the curious, the believers and the skeptics, the grateful and the broken.

Why do you think we hear this Gospel so often? What is it calling us to? Why do Scripture scholars tell us this Gospel has Eucharistic roots?

The scene on that grassy plain is supposed to mirror the gathering at this table today. In the loaves and the fish, Jesus transforms a crowd of all ages, talents, abilities and backgrounds into a community of generosity. Does it mirror our Eucharist today? Does our Eucharist transform us and our world? What can we do to make sure it does?

Our Eucharistic community should reflect the diversity on that hillside. Does it? Or have we become a comfortable community of like-minded fellow travelers who pride ourselves on singing "All are Welcome" as long as some of them don't really show up?

That is the challenge of the Gospel. That is the mandate of the Eucharist foreshadowed in this miracle story: to take up the hard work of reconciliation, inclusiveness and compassion…to do the difficult task of evangelization. It is not just about taking up OUR spot at the picnic.

That hillside miracle along with our Eucharist is possible only when self defers to community, only when serving others is exalted over being served, only when differences dissolve, only when the so called critics and fringe people are pulled into the circle, only when the common and the shared are honored above opinion, status, orthodoxy and comfort.

That is the hard work of Eucharist.

It is the heart of who we are.

Eighteenth Sunday in Ordinary Time (A)
Matthew 14:13-21

Today's readings, especially the Gospel, are about community and justice. Both of those concepts are challenging to the point of being rejected by many so-called Christians today.

Let's consider these two concepts separately.

First, COMMUNITY. Imagine a scenario like this, right here at St. Luke. (It is not hard because it has happened.) A young man in the parish or maybe a beloved charter member dies. Parishioners quietly go to work organizing donations of salads, casseroles, bread, and all kinds of desserts for a wonderful luncheon in the parish hall.

A lot of people come to the funeral and join their hearts and voices with the grieving family. That's why we call people when one of us dies. And then the Eucharist they bless, break and share at the altar inspires the luncheon that follows. The Christ who multiplied the bread and fish on the hillside, who transformed simple bread and wine into the very life of God at the Last Supper, now works a new miracle: Christ multiplies their pasta salads and macaroni casseroles, prepared out of compassion into something sacred in which God is present again to grieving families and friends who hurt with them.

The "leftovers" aren't just food, but baskets full of the grace and consolation that bind people together. They break bread and share the cup and while still hurting and grieving, find peace and harmony.

Eucharist is an act of giving and receiving. The early Church saw the miracle of today's Gospel as a precursor of the Eucharist. Jesus begins with collecting what people are willing to give—a few pieces of bread and fish—and gives them back to the givers. It seems like a picnic, but it is really Eucharist. Jesus not only increases the food but transforms the givers into a community…a community of many different souls who become one in their need, one in the bread they share, one in the love of Christ.

Christ EMPOWERS each one of us to perform our own miracles. It is about community. Some people won't like this! But do you know what that makes Jesus? A community leader, an organizer. Only in the world of politics has that become a bad word!

Jesus inspires us to take on the work of the gospel: to feed the hungry, to care for the sick, to lift up the fallen. Indeed, this Gospel is about community.

Now for the second part: JUSTICE. No one knows for sure, but the United Nations' Food and Agriculture Organization estimates there to be 925 million hungry people in the world. That is one out of every seven. Most are in Asia and the Pacific or Africa, Latin America, and the Caribbean. Nineteen million are in so-called developed countries like our own. And the number of hungry people is increasing.

Hunger was no stranger in the days of Isaiah and Jesus. Isaiah wrote of people longing to be filled. In the Gospel, Jesus enacts God's promise to fill the hungry. But do you know what? Jesus' act of heartfelt compassion for the crowds was also a politically subversive action. It is a big part of what got him killed.

In Jesus' day, as now, food was about power. The rich were about 2% of the population and they controlled the food. The rest struggled daily to feed themselves. Taxes, pestilence and drought ate up their resources and left them on the brink of starvation.

In today's world, there is easily enough food for everyone and then some. In the Gospel, Jesus' disciples presume there is enough food for everyone, but they figure it is someone else's responsibility to provide it. They want to send the crowd somewhere else to procure it. ("Let them get it in the villages!")

But Jesus directs them to a solution that (again) depends on remaining in community and pooling and distributing their resources. Community and justice.

In a Eucharistic action he transforms all that they have and there is enough. And Matthew's note that the 5,000 did not include women and children is a keen reminder that children and their mothers are still the hardest hit by hunger.

The Gospel invites us to justice, to resist the politically suicidal temptation to consider it someone else's responsibility.

When we gather at Eucharist, we not only give thanks but seek to understand the causes of hunger and redouble our efforts. Such actions provoke opposition from those who benefit from hunger and the unequal distribution of food. And don't be naïve. There are those who benefit from someone else's hunger. In the 1950s Jesus' actions would have gotten him called a Communist. Today, what he did might be called socialist. You see, we manage to ignore the Gospel by politicizing everything and redefining good words into something bad.

After the execution of John the Baptist, Jesus fed the crowds, knowing he could be the next victim of Rome. But it was about community and justice and he would not be deterred.

It is no accident that those gatherings after a funeral are called mercy meals. If we can come together in COMMUNITY to prepare food to share at a time of grieving and hurting, we can also come together in JUSTICE to feed the poor of the world.

Eighteenth Sunday in Ordinary Time (B)
John 6:24-35

As I noted with last Sunday's Gospel of the multiplication of the loaves and fishes, we have begun a series of Sundays which focus entirely on the Bread of Life discourses in John's Gospel.

Tomorrow, we will have Mass here with some 400 people who will be celebrating a Jubilee for the Ursuline Sisters. In reflecting on how the ministry of the nuns has changed and developed over the years, I got to thinking of how it has changed for all of you...for all of us. And it all flows from Eucharist.

—It is nourished by Eucharist.

—It is inspired by Eucharist.

—And it is all Spirit driven.

Think of some of the ecclesial ministries that lay people commit themselves to today, ministries that your grandparents and even your parents would never have thought of.

Think about it. You are ministers of the Eucharist, you proclaim the Word, and you engage in all liturgical ministries. (Our mothers and grandmothers were allowed to scrub the altar.) You serve on Pastoral Council and work on evangelization. You oversee the finances of the parish. You work at the Dorothy Day House and the Rescue Mission. You raise money and have a say in how it is spent. You are lay leaders of prayer and engage in faith formation like Seeking Christ and Awakening Faith. (Your fathers were allowed to teach CCD.) You facilitate prayer groups and engage in faith sharing. You bake Communion bread and take the Blessed Sacrament to the sick and homebound. You know more Scripture than your grandparents were ever exposed to and you have taken in God's Word better than any evangelical. I can't make an exhaustive list of all the ministries.

The point is, every shred of that work and ministry is the real presence of Christ initiated in Eucharist and released into the world by your commitment.

117

See if the Bread of Life discourses in these Gospels don't sound like Jesus had today's Church in mind. Last week when he created a community out of a diverse crowd on a hillside with just a few loaves and fish from one small boy? And again, today when he promises a bread that will feed all our hungers?

Yes, we have problems in the Church. There have always been problems in the church starting with Peter and Paul. It is because it is made up of human beings. But in spite of those problems, the people of God forge ahead and make progress, sometimes in spite of poor leadership. And do you know why? It is because of Eucharist, the Bread of Life. It is because of people like you, steeped in our true Eucharistic tradition rather than stunted liturgical practice.

It is because, most of the time, you know how to bring the face of Christ and the presence of Christ to others through your ministries and everyday life.

Do you get lazy sometimes? Yes. Do you mess up sometimes? Of course. So did the greatest saints. But ultimately, you get it.

In this Eucharist, we become the Body of Christ. To a world shrouded in materialism and pessimism, we bring the light of Christ…from this table.

To a world imprisoned by terror and conjured-up fear, we bring the freedom of Christ…from this table.

To a world hurting and dying, we bring the wounded Christ…from this table.

We carry, from this table, Christ's works of mercy…Christ's voice of forgiveness…Christ's deeds of compassion.

It is here, in this Eucharist, the sign of God's abundance, where our hungers are fed, our hearts are nourished, our ministry is inspired, our Good News is affirmed, and our work begins.

When I was first asked to preside at this Mass, I was thinking that Pauline and Patricia and Kathleen could have found either a fresh face or a "wisdom figure" to celebrate with all of you today. Then someone said to me, "Maybe you are a wisdom figure." That was upsetting! To be a wisdom figure at my young age! So, I was going for "fresh" when I remembered Sister Carmel telling me over 50 years ago in 6th grade, "Don't get fresh with me young man." So, I scuttled that idea too.

Then I got the letter from Mary McCormick instructing me that the Jubilarians did not want me to expound on their personal achievements (of which there are many) or prepare premature eulogies (which none of us are ready for.) They just wanted me to preach the Gospel informed by my own prayer and reflection. The ultimate affirmation and challenge. So here goes...

With last Sunday's Gospel of the multiplication of the loaves and fishes, we have begun a series of Sundays which focus entirely on the Bread of Life discourses in John's Gospel. And that is perfect for what we are here to do today.

Eucharist is first, the center of all the various ministries we represent. It is second the lynchpin on which hang all of our meager and noble efforts to preach and live the Good News, the gospel.

First, various ministries, without expounding on personal achievements. The ministries of the Ursuline Sisters have grown and expanded, even as numbers declined. That is Spirit-driven. Most of us can remember the day when every nun you knew either taught school or worked in the hospital. Now, I would have a hard time listing all the work that is being done. I think every shred of that work is the real presence of Christ initiated in Eucharist and released into the world by dedicated, committed and competent men and women who know how to be Eucharist in the most challenging situations.

Don't the Bread of Life discourses of Jesus sound like he had today's Church and specifically today's women religious in mind as he created a community out of a diverse crowd with a few loaves and fish from one small boy? And then again in today's Gospel promise of a bread that will feed ALL our hungers.

It is true, as Notre Dame Sister Mary Maher says, "that not all have arrived at a level of comfort recognizing a truly APOSTOLIC, and not monastic, religious life, especially for women." But the solid support for women religious in the face of recent paranoia and silliness from Rome proves that many in the Church and in the world are more than comfortable. And I would offer that those steeped in our true Eucharistic tradition rather than stunted liturgical practice get it. And they recognize the face and presence of Christ in ministries that push the envelope and reach the real needs of real people. So, your ministries.

Second, our meager and noble efforts to preach the gospel. And I feel competent to speak about this relative to the Ursuline Sisters because, like countless other people, including so many of the priests in America, I was formed by the Good News as it was preached and lived and developed by the Ursuline Sisters over the decades of my life and beyond. They have lived and preached the Good News for every era they have spanned.

It was an African American woman, who, although not a nun, capsulized what I had learned from Grade One at Sacred Heart School. She said, "I am not here to preach good times. No, I'm here to preach Good News." And indeed, we are.

The Good News that in both youthful enthusiasm and in aging wisdom, we are anointed for the poor and the marginalized and the forgotten.

The Good News that to a world shrouded in dark materialism and blinded by a crisis of leadership, we offer sight and vision.

The Good News that in spite of orchestrated death, we will release those imprisoned by institutionalized terror and conjured up fear.

The Good News that we have the awesome responsibility and unique privilege to carry the wounded Christ to a hurting world.

The Good News that we carry in our hands, works of mercy…we carry in our voices, words of forgiveness…we carry in our hearts, deeds of compassion.

Oh yes, you know well it is not always good times. But it is always Good News.

Indeed, the Ursulines and I and all of you have been celebrating the Good News for a long time (not just 50 years) and in lots of ways for lots of reasons.

It is here, in this Eucharist, the sign of God's abundance, where our hungers are fed, our hearts are nourished, our ministry is inspired, our Good News is affirmed, and our work begins.

I didn't do this in my homily, but it is appropriate now without expounding on personal achievements or edging into premature eulogies that I can say to all the Ursulines:

Thank you for forming the faith of generations.

Thank you for living on the edge.

Thank you for giving birth to new relationships.

Thank you for being more than unpaid workers in a
    hierarchical project.

Thank you for working for justice.

Thank you for standing with the victimized.

Thank you for being intellectuals, scholars and artists.

Thank you for spiritual wisdom and your search for meaning.

Thank you for looking for love.

Thank you for unfathomable abundance.

Assumption of Mary (A)
Luke 1:39-56

Caryll Houselander was an English mystic and poet who was born in the early 1900s. Though she was untrained, doctors sent patients to her for counseling during World War II. One doctor said that because Caryll saw Christ suffering in every person, she was able to love them back to life.

She wrote extensively about the Blessed Virgin Mary and she gives us some important thoughts to contemplate on today's feast.

Here is why we celebrate Mary today:

"In a cold cave in a Palestinian backwater, she cradled her child. After a long, hard journey, she joyfully welcomed the child Messiah. The circle of her loving arms changed this lost sorrowful world forever. Years later, on that horrible Friday, she stood by her son in his final moments. Betrayed and abandoned by his friends, abused and condemned for speaking of a loving God, he was crucified. Before his body was consigned to a grave, she cradled it one last time.

"But the woman called to be the Mother of God, was first a child of God, like each of us. Today we celebrate that the God she welcomed into her world has now welcomed her into his. The Christ who held her hand as a boy, has taken her hand and led her into a heavenly dwelling place. Her song—the lullaby that rocked the Christ child to sleep, the tearful goodbye she whispered as they laid him in the garden—now comforts this confused, lost and angry world, if we would only let our ears hear it."

As she welcomed the Christ child, so we are called to do, wherever we find him.

As she journeyed with her son to Jerusalem, so we are called to take up our cross and follow him.

As she held the broken body of her son, we are called to hold and support and heal one another in our brokenness.

Today we do not only celebrate Mary being united with her Son in heaven, but the possibility for all of us to share that joy.

122

Twentieth Sunday in Ordinary Time (B)
John 6:51-58

Many of us remember and lived through the day when the Eucharist was all tabernacles and locked golden doors and benediction and "Lord I am not worthy." Some may think they long for those days when Eucharist was an object outside ourselves. But that understanding of Eucharist was an institutional limitation imposed by a frightened Church in reaction to the Protestant Reformation. It was circling the wagons. It was more about institutional control than faith and sacrament. It was defensive and narrow. But all that external stuff is not what Jesus meant when he said, "Eat my body...drink my blood."

It is certainly not at all what John the Evangelist has been presenting to us over the past few weeks. What John has presented is at once messy and challenging, pure and comforting. It is about picnics and leftover baskets. It is about confused disciples growing in love for Jesus and one another. It is about a certainly mixed and often unruly crowd. It is about people arguing and demanding signs of Jesus. It is about Jesus meeting people where they were. It is about Jesus knowing what people need better than they know themselves. It is at once about real bread and nourishment, but also about seeing beyond the bread and wine, seeing beyond what we can touch, seeing into a Great Mystery.

Today, John makes it clear that Eucharist is not and never should have been a remote ritual or a sacred artifact to be adored, but it is real bread, real food. In fact, Eucharist won't work if it is all about rules and rubrics. It must be vibrant, not boring. It is living. It is never static, never passive. In fact, if you think of Eucharist as you did when you were seven, then you are stuck. Eucharist is a growing gift. It changes us. It brings us together in the midst of our busy-ness. It is real bread that nurtures the love of God. Once that is understood and embraced, no one can be judged unworthy by another. No one can be excluded.

John makes it clear that we don't get Eucharist because we are worthy, we get Eucharist because we are hungry…hungry for the Living Christ, hungry for real food, hungry for all God has to offer us.

To receive Eucharist, we need to open our hands and let go of anxieties, fears, sins and judgment. We need to open our hands and take the bread that is the life and love of God.

Yet Eucharist demands more than just the opening our hands to take and our mouths to consume. It demands that we open our hearts and spirits as well so that we may become what we receive. In inviting us to feed on his flesh and drink his blood, Jesus is really calling us to become his life of compassion and reconciliation and mercy. You can't do that with clenched fists and closed minds and locked hearts and institutional in-fighting. It won't work.

In offering himself as our food, Jesus is not inviting us into an arrangement of distant, if respectful prayer. He is not inviting us into some devotional desert. He is inviting us into community and a love so intimate that we become what we eat. We consume, not Jesus of Nazareth, but the cosmic, resurrected Christ…the whole church…the very heart of God.

Twenty-First Sunday in Ordinary Time (A)
Matthew 16:13-20

Today's Gospel only works (of course) if you take it personally. The question, "Who do you say that I am?" leads right into another question, often asked of us, "Why are you here?" or "Why do you stay in the Church?" I need to let Jesus ask me that first question every day. "Who do you say that I am?" And the answer makes me stay, makes me push on, calls me to be faithful.

And I take great comfort in the fact that it was Peter who answered the question rightly. Peter! A couple of weeks ago he lost faith and started sinking in the water. Jesus took his hand.

This week, Peter is spot on with his answer: "You are the Christ, the Son of the Living God." And Jesus gives him authority, the keys to the kingdom, not as a personal possession as some leaders have thought, but as a communal treasure that gives everyone access. Jesus says, "Blessed are you."

Next week Jesus will call Peter, Satan...an obstacle. What a roller coaster ride for Peter. And yet, he remains the image of the Church, the Rock. It can be a roller coaster ride for all of us. I take comfort in that. It is OK to make myself vulnerable. I am in the good company of many good people who have admitted they are sinners and have doubted and have stayed.

When I look around and see so many of my colleagues who have left ministry and often the Church, I do wonder why I am here. When I look around and see so many of your family and friends and fellow Catholics missing, I wonder why I am here. But then Jesus' question comes searing into my brain. It is like he is saying, "Look at me...Look me in the eye...Stay focused. Who do YOU say that I am?"

There are many times when the negative stuff and the problems challenge my faith and I want to run:

When thousands of children were raped around the world and when men of power, so called bishops ignored their cries...

When women are marginalized and sidelined and their creativity is wasted...

When entire communities are denied Eucharist because of blind faithfulness to meaningless rules...

When power and greed and corruption appear in the highest levels of Church and government...

But then I think of Jesus' question: "Who do you say that I am?" and ask myself, in the words of Brian Doyle, spiritual essayist and editor, "what sort of rat leaves the ship when it is foundering and my fellow passengers need help? How could I leave the ship in the hands of men who nearly sank her? How could I abandon the brave, the honest mothers and priests and nuns and teachers and bishops and popes and dads and monks and children who are the church...who sing the deepest, holiest song of the real church?"

Because, you see, there really are others who answer the question, "Who do you say that I am?" They won't let the light of Christ and the idea of Church be snuffed out. They refuse to let incompetent leadership and selfishness define who they are.

There are people like Dorothy Day and Mother Teresa and Pope Francis and Thomas Merton and Richard Rohr and Annie Dillard who help me stay focused because they have answered the question.

I stay because this is a church where born and unborn children, where young soldiers and disenfranchised prisoners, where old prostitutes and wise men and women, where defiant teens and terminally-ill patients are all held in esteem and have worth and are embraced by Christ.

This is Christ's Church, where, if we stand together and stop fussing about power and words and real estate and rules, we can be instruments of transformation.

"Who do you say that I am?" Indeed! You are the one who pours millions of quiet, gracious miracles into our lives. You are the one who defies reason and logic and relies on imagination, hunger for truth and love. You are the Christ.

126

Twenty-First Sunday in Ordinary Time (B)
John 6:60-69

There is a prevailing sadness in today's Gospel. Jesus' words about being the "bread of life" alienate many. Like all of us at times, Peter and the rest of the twelve are struggling to remain faithful...to make sense of Jesus...to understand and accept his Word. And don't underestimate the disappointment Jesus felt. Being God did not spare him the full range of human emotions including sadness, especially when he saw his friends walk away. We don't usually think of Jesus and his disciples being caught up in emotions. But they were.

The new Pixar film *Inside Out* has excellent insight into that very thing. It tells the story of Riley Anderson, a happy, bright child. She is outgoing, smart and a terrific hockey player. The film takes the viewer on a tour through the mind of eleven-year-old Riley.

A friend dragged me to see it. I protested that it was an animated children's film that would not interest me. Turned out that, although little ones might be entertained by the animation and the characters, the film was quite adult in its message.

It tells Riley's story from an unusual perspective. As I said, the story unfolds in the mind of Riley. We watch the animated characters of her emotions: Joy, Sadness, Anger, Disgust and Fear. The emotions in this movie are more than theories. These emotions both cooperate and fight with one another over the control panel of her brain as Riley struggles through life.

In a wonderfully imaginative way, the film shows how the trail of our life is determined, not by the raw misfortunes or blessings we experience but by how we respond to them.

The most surprising realization of this film is the reality that Joy and Sadness are not rivals, but partners. We all want Joy to guide our lives, but in truth Sadness is the greater teacher. Sadness helps us realize what our lives truly long for. Sadness enables us to change directions when necessary. Sadness empowers us to respond to the plight of others with empathy because we know how it feels.

There is a beautiful moment in the film when Sadness sits down next to a character who is hurting. Joy just wants to cheer him up. But Sadness sits down next to him and helps him embrace his situation and move beyond despondency.

Obviously, we all prefer Joy. Joy is the confidence that says, "We can fix this" or "We can do it." But it is our ability to FEEL sad that stirs compassion in others and empathy within ourselves.

There is no growth without loss. There is no progress without longing. Like all of us, Riley and her family rediscover Joy in their lives once Sadness is acknowledged and allowed to take command of the control panel for the moment.

So, there is a Sadness in today's Gospel as Jesus and the faithful few watch others walk away. For the disciples, that prevailing Sadness leads to the Joy of embracing the Eucharist, allowing it to knit their lives together, heal their hurts and connect them forever to Jesus. Sadness can do the same for us.

Just as that emotion helps Riley and her folks realize what has gone wrong and restore a sense of Joy to their lives, just as the sadness that Jesus and his disciples experience enabled them to continue their journey with new understanding, so with us. Acknowledging our Sadness in the context of Eucharist gives us a depth of understanding and, yes, even Joy.

That's why we need Eucharist every week and even every day. It guides us through emotional roller coasters and even depressing challenges. It is a guaranteed mystical experience that can put everything into perspective, if only we allow it.

Twenty-Second Sunday in Ordinary Time (A)
Matthew 16:21-27

I read in *America* magazine that the women of La Paz, Bolivia suffered because of a total misunderstanding of today's Gospel. One woman recounts that at one time they strongly identified with the crucified Christ. The women lived with a strong sense of submission. They submitted to sexual abuse from their fathers, uncles and husbands, thinking that whatever suffering they endured they did so as their way of carrying the cross with Jesus. Now we immediately recognize this as absurdity to the point of sacrilege.

However, these women went through a process of learning and became aware that they were lovable and precious in God's eyes. They recognized that a misreading of this Gospel had obliterated their sense of self and kept them from embracing their real call. They realized that Jesus was intent on lifting up those who were bowed down and on healing all who suffered. Once they did that, they were able to question and challenge the so-called wisdom they had received for generations.

Submitting to abuse and injustice is just the opposite of identifying with Christ. At one extreme, Jesus is not encouraging us to put up with sinful situations in some misguided effort to suffer with him. At the other extreme, he is not suggesting that we forego some pleasure (like eating chocolate during Lent) and claim that by doing so we are identifying with Christ. And all those little, inconsequential things that we were told to "offer up" don't come close to suffering with Jesus.

No, Jesus is referring to a disciple's choice to lose himself or herself, to take on Christ's way of life, to take on Christ's mission, to fight against injustice, to speak up in the name of peace, to take a stand against what is sinful. It has nothing to do with suffering silently. It has everything to do with centering on the love of God expressed through more than rule-keeping but through prayer, service and action in the name of the kingdom. If you suffer repercussions for taking the risk to live as Jesus did, then that is the cross.

Another valid approach to this Gospel is reinterpreting our lives in the face of bad events. Recently, thousands of people lost their life savings in Bernie Madoff's 65 billion-dollar Ponzi scheme. One woman recounts how, in losing everything, they also lost their attachment to what they THOUGHT they needed to be happy. She says that, before they lost their savings, she was always complaining about her house, she didn't like the way her husband ate his cereal or wore ankle socks with his shorts, and she especially didn't like the way he was always focusing on the positive. She goes on to say that after Madoff confessed, it seemed miraculous that she was married for more than 20 years to a man she loved. From the perspective of losing everything, having ANYTHING seems like winning the lottery.

Today's Gospel is not about rolling over and playing dead in the face of adversity. Jesus challenges us to re-evaluate our distorted relationships, whether with people, with money, with food, with technology, with sports or with pursuits that eat up our lives at the expense of what is truly important: family, friends and GOD.

Jesus asked his disciples and us to detach from what is shallow and worthless to embrace the lasting, fulfilling things of God. If we are true to Jesus' call to discipleship, if we embrace the cross, then we should find ourselves embracing values that run counter to what society honors. We will turn from grudge-keeping and embrace reconciliation. We will call war evil and embrace peace-making. We will put aside our own wants for what is best for family and community.

As disciples, we take up the cross, not out of a sense of self-loathing…not out of a misguided interpretation of what has always been…not out of a sense of pessimism or apathy but out of a sense of conviction and hope that the demands of the gospel and the cross will result in a life of LOVE and PROMISE.

Twenty-Second Sunday in Ordinary Time (B)
Mark 7:1-8, 14-15, 21-23

There is a story about a great warrior in Ancient China. He abandoned his life of war and destruction and became a monk. He happily lived a quiet life serving his brother monks and the poor and the sick of the villages around the monastery.

One day an arrogant warrior rode through the village. He terrorized and abused the villagers. Then he made his way to the monastery where he recognized the monk from their former days of pillaging and plunder. The abusive warrior was angry at the passivity of the monk, ridiculed him and did everything he could to provoke his old adversary. But the monk would not respond. Finally, the warrior grew tired of the game. He defiantly spat on the door of the monastery and rode off.

The villagers who had been brutalized by the warrior, asked the monk why he did not confront his old enemy and defend them.

The wise monk asked, "If someone offers you a gift and you do not accept it, to whom does the gift belong?"

They replied, "It belongs to the one who offered it."

The wise monk said, "The same is true for anger, ridicule and envy. When they are not accepted, they forever belong to the one who holds on to them."

We know that. In the hurts, indignities and injustices perpetrated against us, as individuals, as a community, as a country, what is often worse than the act itself is what the act does to us: we often respond with suspicion, cynicism, anger, vengeance and retaliation. That hurts us more than it hurts our so-called enemies.

One of the most difficult challenges to being a disciple of Jesus is NOT to let those things "outside" of us diminish who we are "inside." When we are attacked, it is difficult NOT to let such anger or vengeance displace the things of God in the sacred place of our hearts. It is difficult but not impossible. Rather than let someone's aggression and hatred transform us into hateful people, let God's presence transform us and the evil around us into compassion and forgiveness.

Think of people you know who hold grudges. What happens to them? Better yet, look into your own heart and see what anger does to you. Why give anyone that much power over you, especially someone who does not care about you? It is one thing to let someone who loves you transform you into a more loving person. It is quite another to let someone who hates you turn you into a hateful person.

The same can be said about our community and our church and our country. When they respond to prejudice and anger and aggression with vengeance, they diminish themselves and the enemy wins.

Here I could go off on a tangent about the social issues, the wars, the life issues and the political issues we respond to badly (abortion, the war, immigration, the environment, the election...). We have a history of responding badly which never solves the problem, improves the situation or makes our lives better. But you can put two and two together. You know better than all the rhetoric being hurled at us.

Jesus says it so well. The evil outside us, the evil that is leveled at us cannot hurt. The evil that comes from within truly defiles us. Jesus invites us to always pursue that safe place, that beautiful place where the goodness that God has placed in our hearts can not only survive but be passed on to others.

Twenty-Third Sunday in Ordinary Time (A)
Matthew 18:15-20

Jesus gives us a double dose today. First, he teaches us how to be a friend. Second, he teaches us how to be church. And they are built on one another.

On being a friend: A college professor was teaching a course on ethics. He shared with his students Aristotle's idea that ethics is rooted in the virtue of friendship. Aristotle's premise was that a true friend has the right to tell you the truth, even when truth-telling can be painful.

The professor asked his students to share stories of ethical dilemmas they had encountered. The professor was struck by the number of stories in which a student AVOIDED challenging a friend who was involved in some hurtful or even self-destructive behavior. The students justified their silence along the lines of: "Who am I to judge?" or "I didn't want to risk our friendship." The professor told his students: "You give friendship a bad name. Whereas Aristotle made friends the basis of ethics, you made friendship the excuse for supporting unethical behavior."

Jesus presents a model of what true friendship should be: trusting enough to challenge each other, caring enough to "risk" the friendship in order to preserve it, realizing that peace is not the absence of conflict, but the presence of justice and compassion. Christ urges us not to tolerate the dysfunction in our lives but to confront with love and understanding the misunderstandings, problems and issues that divide us and embitter us. He calls us to be committed to seek solutions to our problems.

That approach can even be applied to all the social and political issues of our day. On this Labor Day weekend, for example, today's Gospel applies directly to the current debate going on about workers' rights and the clash between unbridled capitalism on one hand and negotiation gone awry on the other, between the oppression of big business vs. the dignity of workers. Why can't we have employment and a sense of responsibility and dignity among workers? Why can't we have corporations who understand their responsibility to give back to the community? Why can't we have a community who lives and works together for the common good in a spirit of mutual respect? Is it gospel? Is it ethics? Is it friendship? Is it all of the above?

The second point of the Gospel is *On Being Church*. One man took a business trip to South America. He visited a small church in one of the poor barrios and was deeply moved by the joy-filled faith of the people who lived in overwhelming poverty. When he returned home, he talked about it with some friends after Mass. They contacted the pastor of the barrio parish. Then they collected school and medical supplies and shipped them. Next, they gathered clothes and linens and shipped those. Now they are raising money to dig a new well for the community. They see themselves as just a group of friends, but they are being church.

There is one parish that has what is known as "THE LIST"— names and phone numbers of folks in the parish who can be called day or night. An elderly parishioner needs a ride to the doctor? Call Susan. She can arrange it. A young couple is struggling through a difficult pregnancy? Sheila and Pat know what to do. Call them. The parents in one family had been out of work for over a year. Now the father finally has a job but the one car they own breaks down and he can't get to work. Neil can handle it. Call him. You see, it is more than a list of numbers. It is church.

Two teenagers had participated in the parish summer Bible School when they were youngsters. Now that they are in high school, they help in July serving as leaders and counselors. The adults responsible for the program tell you immediately that these teens make the program **work.** They are church.

When Jesus says in the Gospel: "Tell the church," it is with a small "c." He is not talking about telling the priests or the bishop or the canon lawyers. He is talking about the people who are the church. It is the other important lesson of today's Gospel: the ability of individuals who come together as disciples to accomplish great works of compassion and justice, even if only two or three.

We are the friends willing to speak up. We are the church willing to pitch in.

That Jesus, how clever was he?

The gospel is always about us, in the best sense.

Twenty-Third Sunday in Ordinary Time (B)
Mark 7:31-37

The meaningless, cacophonous babble of our noise-saturated society has made many of us deaf to others and to the world. At the same time, our contentiously divided and angry world has rendered many of us silent. We have iPhones and GPS systems that talk to us, but we don't listen or speak to one another.

In today's Gospel, Jesus says, EPHPHATHA—BE OPENED. We would do well to make it a mantra-like prayer for our lives. If you like the Greek say, EPHPHATHA. If you're content with English say, BE OPENED. Pray it over and over again, every day. When Jesus said it, the man was healed. He could speak and hear where before he was deaf and dumb. It is a reminder that we can be healed by it too.

We need the prayer. We need to learn how to speak once again, words of truth, healing and peace. We need learn how to listen again to God and to one another.

In today's Gospel Jesus calls us to BE OPENED. That is to listen and to speak. But also to be opened by the possibilities of transformation.

In times of sickness, grief, fear, despair and frustration we can be "deaf" to the presence of God, isolating ourselves from God's compassion when we need it most. We close our ears and our mouths. We block up our hearts and our minds. We need to make EPHPHATHA—BE OPENED our prayer.

This week is the anniversary of 9/11, a good time to initiate the prayer to BE OPENED.

Many of you may remember that fatality #1 on 9/11 was Father Mychal Judge. Including him, over 3,000 were butchered by evil that day. But do you know how he died? He was hit by flying debris when he took off his helmet so he could hear the dying words of the man he was anointing.

What have we done since that devastating, tragic day? We have figured out new ways to put our helmets on and stop listening and speaking to one another.

135

We have closed our national ear to the cry of the sick, the aging, the poor and the unborn. We have closed our communal heart to the power of love and forgiveness. We have shut our ecclesial mouth, refusing to speak words of welcome and peace to the very ones Jesus sought out. We have closed our national borders to people like our own ancestors who are looking for freedom and a chance to contribute to the success of a nation. We have closed our minds to possibilities of growth and change as we claw for wealth and prosperity.

Oh yes, we have rebuilt the buildings of 9/11, but we have failed to rebuild a country based on truth and justice. We have mourned and buried the dead of that horrible day, but we do injustice to their memory by allowing the evil of terrorism to win out by turning us into something ugly at worst and indifferent at best.

We elect leaders because they feed our fear and our selfishness and push us toward exclusivity and narrowness. We go to churches that proclaim a gospel of prosperity on one hand or quibble over words on the other, with no challenge to outreach, openness and radical change.

BE OPENED indeed. Do you realize that the Gospel of Jesus Christ has the answers we are looking for and the marching orders we need? We need to listen. We need to speak. *Ephphatha. Ephphatha.* Keep saying it until it happens. Be opened. Be opened.

Twenty-Fifth Sunday in Ordinary Time (A)
Matthew 20:1-16a

Almost everyone has the same reaction to this parable. And so it does what any good parable must do: shake us loose, confront us with something we don't like and make us re-think whatever it is we thought we knew. Almost everyone thinks, at first glance, that it seems unfair. But we know at some deeper level that it must be calling us to a different perspective, a new way of seeing.

The vineyard owner's question is key. In our translation the owner asks, "Are you envious because I am generous?" But the literal translation is this: "Is your eye evil because I am good." The question points out the destructiveness of evil-eye envy in a community. Some grew up knowing about the threat of the evil eye (*malocchio*). We need a new perspective, a new way of seeing, a good eye.

Listen to this Arabian folk tale. A man walking through the forest saw a fox that had lost its hind legs. He wondered how the poor animal could survive. Then he saw a tiger come into the clearing with game in its mouth. The tiger ate its fill and then left the rest of the meat for the fox. The next day God fed the fox by means of the same tiger.

The man marveled at God's great compassion and said to himself, "I too shall just sit here like the crippled fox, in full trust in the Lord that he will provide me with what I need."

The man remained in the forest for several days. But nothing happened. The poor man was almost at death's door from hunger when he heard a voice saying, "Oh, you poor fool. Open your eyes to the truth. Stop imitating the disabled fox and instead, be like the tiger."

Oh yes, the Gospel calls us to a new perspective, a new way of seeing. It calls us to set aside our evil eye. We can become too preoccupied with our disappointment at what has failed us, too overwhelmed by our anger over what has hurt us, too debilitated by our own cynicism and self-important sense of fairness.

God's unconditional, extravagant love cannot be restricted by our human ways of thinking. Thank God. God's generosity, love and forgiveness are so over the top that they often offend our sense of carefully timed and measured justice, our sense of what we think we have earned. Indeed, it is all grace. Whether your commitment is long-lived and faithful or whether it is new and exciting, it is all gift.

This is a great parable precisely because it smacks us in the face. Most of us are prone to compare ourselves to the ones who worked all day. Some of us may compare ourselves to the ones who came at the last minute. Remember the fox and the tiger.

This parable works because, after we fussed and discussed and thought about all the unfairness and unexpected luck of some people, we can be hit with the staggering truth that we are called to be the tiger. This Gospel is not about what is fair and just. This Gospel is not about a stroke of good luck that puts us first. This Gospel is about imitating God's love, generosity and compassion. "Getting it" may take a lifetime.

A few years ago, poet and activist Fr. Daniel Berrigan spoke at the University of Notre Dame about his ministry at a hospice for the terminally ill. Each week he would go to spend some time by the bed of a young boy who was completely incapacitated, physically and mentally. The boy could only lie there, mute and helpless and totally unable to communicate.

Berrigan said he would sit by the boy to "hear" what the boy was saying in his silence and helplessness. For Berrigan, the way this child lies in our world is the way God lies in our world. To hear what God is saying, we must learn to hear what this child is saying.

We want God to be the magic man, the one who smashes our problems and supports our bias. But God's presence does not overpower anyone or anything. God's presence lies quietly at the deep moral and spiritual base of things. It does not overpower with strength or attractiveness or brilliance or intelligence. While it is possible to behold God in strength or beauty or brilliance or swiftness, God is first revealed in the silence of humility and simplicity and peace—in the silence and vulnerability of a child.

That was Berrigan's point. The child represents for the disciple of Jesus, the vulnerabilities and fears and doubts that everyone of us experiences in our lives. And the child reminds us of Jesus' call to take up his work of reaching out to those overwhelmed by such anxiety and despair. In the service we give and the respect we afford to others, Jesus says we welcome into our midst the very presence of God.

There is a parallel point to this. On the final exam in a psychology course taught at the University of Maryland, the professor, Dr. Dylan Selterman, poses this as the last question: "Select whether you want two points or six points added to your final grade. But there is a small catch: If more that 10% of the class selects six points, then no one gets any points."

How would you have answered? Well, 20% selected six points so, true to his word, the professor gave no extra credit to anyone.

139

What was the point? The professor explains that the question is intended to illustrate the dilemma between doing what's good for you as an individual versus doing what's best for the group. It's true that many people behave selfishly. But if too many people behave selfishly, the group will suffer...and then everyone in the group individually will suffer.

In the seven years that he has used this question, self-interest has trumped the common good. Dr. Selterman believes that most students select the six-point option by way of a "go big or go home" mentality which we see in our culture, in business, in the Church, in politics, in sports. Most people want "their own place in the sun" without regard for others. Most businesses are geared to crush the competitors. Too many churchmen seek their own advancement. Political candidates pursue their own glory rather than the common good. (We are being inundated with this right now, candidates seeking their own glory rather than the common good. I cannot tell you how to vote, but let me give you an early hint: DO NOT vote for one who is just seeking glory. If that is all you've got, then write in your grandmother's name!!) Most players on a team pursue their own scholarship, their own branding, their own success in spite of the cliché that there is no "I" in team.

The extra credit question is analogous to any resource in the world: opportunity, position, food, water, land. If people are mindful of their consumption, then it is fine. But if too many people are selfish, they deprive others but, ironically, in the long run, they also shoot themselves in the foot. And no one wins. Why can't we understand that going for the six-point extra credit option makes us losers?

This is the same lesson Fr. Berrigan learned at the bedside of the child: in the service and care we render to others, especially children, the vulnerable, the rejected and the poor, we welcome into our midst the very presence of God, which brings with it abundance and blessing for all.

It is safe to say that we have no trouble with the gospel point that God expects a commitment and action, not mere words. But then Jesus takes it a giant leap forward and tells the respectable leaders of the people that "prostitutes and tax collectors are entering the kingdom of God before you."

As if last week's Gospel wasn't bad enough with the one who worked only one hour being equal to those who put in a full day! Now this! At some level, we realize the gauntlet that Jesus is throwing down before us. Silently, at some level we reject it. We don't like it.

It is not even that the tax collectors and prostitutes MIGHT or COULD or WILL go into the kingdom before you. No, they ARE entering the kingdom of God before you.

It is not even what we would like to think. They could get into the kingdom if they repent…if they change their ways…if they have a conversion. From our position of security and smugness we love to set up rules and parameters. But Jesus didn't do that. He didn't create any barriers.

Just like saying the words, "Yes, I will go into the vineyard…" doesn't get it. So, WORDS like compassion, forgiveness and mercy are only words until we give full expression to those values in our relationships.

It is not like the old TV show where the contestant was asked, "Is that your final answer?" The Christ in our midst is not looking for the final answer but a final and on-going action.

Too often religious people have all the right answers and fail to see the need to make changes and ACT differently. Religious people want to "stay and keep." You know, "stay" where they are and "keep" what they've got. It is a pitfall for comfortable Christians.

But the father didn't tell his children to stay and keep. He told them to go and work.

The religious people of Jesus' time wouldn't budge, even though they knew better. And so it is for many so-called religious people today.

We seem to have a parallel situation today in the Church. Some Catholics, including some high-ranking leaders in the Church, don't like Pope Francis' message of mercy delivered with good humor. They keep trying to push whatever he says and does into their old categories. They are the ones who claim to have the Good News but about whom Francis says, "They look like someone coming back from a funeral."

Isn't it odd that the right wing in the Church often finds itself in the same camp as the radical right-wing extremists in politics? They want to get rid of this guy who acts on compassion and mercy. They want the old answers, the old securities, the old divisions. They think that is how they get their identity. But the master isn't waiting for old answers. He is looking for new actions.

We always thought that "when the saints go marching in" it would be clear who was who. Turns out the parade is going to be longer than we thought. And maybe, if we are lucky, we will be at the tail-end.

Twenty-Sixth Sunday in Ordinary Time (B)
Mark 9:38-43, 45, 47-48

"We saw someone driving out demons in your name, and we tried to prevent him because he does not follow US." One commentator said that, although we see that kind of tattling as ironic, we are the same way. We see how stupid it was for Jesus' disciples to stop someone from doing good when they themselves frequently messed up when it came to following Jesus. And so do we, still.

Most of the time, it is really only a minority of us (so-called Christians) who really get the true gospel. And count on this, the one who makes the most noise about getting it, usually doesn't! Beware of the person who claims to be promoting gospel or Christian values.

Fr. Richard Rohr says that most of us just keep worshiping Jesus and arguing over the exact right way to do it. The amazing thing is Jesus NEVER ONCE says "worship me!" But he often says, "follow me." There is a difference. And it is usually the case again that the one who "worships" him the loudest, follows him the least.

Being a Christian is a way of life, not a proclamation of beliefs, judgments and rules. Jesus came not just to save us but to show us how to live and love. We have turned Christianity into a formal established religion in order to avoid the demanding lifestyle required by Jesus. That way, we can do what we want and profess creeds at the same time. We can be warlike, greedy, racist, selfish, and vain and still easily believe that "Jesus is my personal Lord and savior." The world has no time for such silliness.

The disciples were trying to hoard their ministry, hoard the gifts that God gives. It happens today (first) in the Church, (second) in public life and (third) in our private lives.

In the Church: When church leaders become more attached to their power and trappings than to seeing the kingdom of God being born wherever possible, it is hoarding ministry. Whether it is the Pope or the bishops or Father Pastor or Pastoral Council or whoever, when there is a hoarding of power and an insistence only on rules, we are no longer following Jesus but our own agenda.

When the wisdom and insight of thoughtful, wise, committed Catholics is overlooked or smothered by edicts from on high, then the kingdom is on hold and Jesus is not being followed. Instead of looking at the divorced, the alienated Catholic, the young, the non-Catholic, the Jew or the Muslim and saying, "Why aren't you one of us…why don't you shape up…why aren't you like us…?" We should be saying, "What are your gifts that the community and the world desperately need?"

In public life: Well, there is no end to the examples here of being far from the requirements that are godly, Christian or biblical. Look at anything: big business, the health-care industry, education, the penal system, the social arena, entertainment, the news media—it is all in shambles. It is all based on who gets the money and who has the power, who controls the cult of celebrity. The common good, the well-being of the poor, the just solution, the gospel demands, or even a good laugh are never considered. It is all about keeping someone else from getting power.

Let me tell you what the gospel demands of you in the current political process. First of all, it demands that you stop using personal diatribes and condemnation and name calling. And if anyone engages in that, turn them off. If anyone says I hate Obama or I despise Romney, that person is neither Christian nor a good citizen. Jesus never condemned a person, not even Judas. He only condemned sin. So, what should we be doing?

Go ahead. Talk politics, talk about ideas, talk about the health care issue, talk about same-sex marriage, talk about the economy. But as soon as the conversation moves from the sharing or debating of ideas into the realm of personal attacks, it is no longer healthy, let alone Christian. Then it is about an ignorant person fed on lying sound bites reserving power and truth to him/herself rather than seeing the good that anyone can offer.

In your private life: And this third one will be brief but no less acceptable to many people. If you are a follower of Jesus, you HAVE no private life in the best sense. You are part of the Body of Christ. And like St. Paul says, "THE HAND CANNOT SAY TO THE FOOT, I DON'T NEED YOU."

What you say behind closed doors, at your family table, on your phone or at your computer, does affect God's world for good or evil. You are not free to say or do whatever you want! Every person has gifts to offer. It is not our job to rip people apart and create division. It is the work of the follower of Jesus to uncover and enable gifts in everyone, just as Jesus did. To do otherwise is to be a liar and thief, robbing the kingdom of all its possibilities. And you are capable of so much more than that.

There are many people who think that, somehow, Scripture and tradition are carved in stone. In today's Gospel we have an example of Jesus taking both into consideration and opening a door so that more people can draw closer to the Lord...so that fewer people can find an excuse to pull away.

Scripture molds how tradition views the world. History and tradition constantly bring different questions and perspectives to Scripture. The Pharisees ask Jesus a question that they knew the answer to. He took them out of their legalistic mindset and moved them into the divine vision of the very nature of the human condition and the marriage relationship.

This homily is not going to go down any of the politically charged roads connected to marriage today: birth control, abortion, same-sex relationships, etc. All those issues are important. But today Jesus invites us to wrestle with the primary issue of marriage in God's plan.

At the same time, he asks us to be sensitive to everyone's pain and the priority of everyone's conscience. Ironically, after one blustering leader declared that the biggest attack on the marriage of man and woman was gay marriage, a comedian countered, "The biggest attack on marriage is not gay marriage but divorce. There are millions more divorces. Let's ban divorce." The obvious irony makes it clear that what needs our attention is the sacredness of marriage rather than the politically charged issues around it.

Jesus neither condemns divorced people nor simply accepts the sad reality of human brokenness. Instead, he suggests that, rather than focusing too quickly on the aftermath of broken relationships with hardened hearts, we recall God's primal plan for human happiness.

In today's reading from Genesis, we are presented with God's final best creation, different from man but wonderfully familiar to him. And suddenly after having named and claimed all the rest of creation, man recognizes his "other self" and bursts forth into the first human words recorded in scripture:

"This one, at last is bone of my bones, flesh of my flesh."

In citing this passage, Jesus appeals above divorce's reality and frequency to the better angels of our nature, thus inspiring his followers. The Church recognizes the mutuality and the dignity of both husband and wife. In the nuptial blessing it says, "may he entrust his heart to her, knowing that she is his equal and joint heir to the life of grace."

Catholic brides are not "given away" by their fathers, and no one says "who gives this woman…" A few brides still want their father to "walk them down the aisle" as they say. But everyone knows that nobody is giving anybody away. Instead, bride and groom each declare their freedom in giving themselves entirely to one another.

And yet, with this struggle to be faithful to Jesus' teaching, the Church also tries to be compassionate toward those whose marriages have broken down, whose love has been betrayed. Although some may make jokes about the Church's annulment process, the meticulous and lengthy procedures testify to the seriousness with which the Church takes Christ's teaching and her concern for members' wholeness and happiness.

If you read a few verses further in today's Genesis passage, after Adam declares Eve to be "flesh of my flesh," you will unfortunately read about the Fall. The couple disobeys God and eats the forbidden fruit. They begin to blame each other. They cover themselves in their shame.

But then comes the Good News, the gospel. Jesus has come into the world to reconcile us to God and to one another. And while someone may reject Jesus, Jesus never rejects anyone. Jesus' whole purpose is to embrace the human situation and find ways to keep people connected to the Father.

147

Twenty-Eighth Sunday in Ordinary Time (A)
Matthew 22:1-14

It occurred to me as I prepared to write this homily, that preaching was a lot easier 40 years ago. Catholics came to church in larger numbers but most of them paid little attention to the Scriptures. And most were certainly not discussing the Bible that much. The priest could get 'em in, tell 'em what he wanted to tell them, they listened or not and everyone sailed along.

Now we have people reading the Bible. We have folks discussing the Scriptures. We have folks weighing in on the parables.

WHAT'S WITH THAT??!!!

Seriously though, what a blessing it is. While our churches may not be overflowing (for lots of reasons), the people who do come are more tuned in. And even the ones who don't come are still searching for answers. In spite of the mounting social problems and moral dilemmas of our culture, those of us who continue to search, really are in a better place spiritually. And for the last few weeks, the parables have caused quite a stir. And we—myself included— have taken steps toward a deeper understanding of what Jesus is saying.

Last week we struggled to understand what it meant to have new tenants in the vineyard. Two weeks ago, we understood about the one son actually DOING his father's will. Before that it was those Johnny-come-lately workers getting paid the same as full-day laborers. And before that it was the master forgiving his servant a huge debt. Today's parable stretches us just as much beyond our sense of what is right and fair.

We get the idea of a generous and loving father preparing a huge banquet. We are not surprised that some don't show up. We even get the image and see Christ in the messengers being beat up and killed. We think it is great that the king sends out to the highways and byways to bring people in. There's a great image of evangelization here.

But then, our sense of fairness and the great American support for the underdog gets all bent out of shape when we perceive that some poor street person is kicked out for not having the right clothes on! We are all set to call the king unfair. He brought him in off the street and now kicks him out for a wardrobe malfunction.

But think again. It is not about proper clothes. It is not about a bag lady needing a Coach purse or an unemployed guy needing a tuxedo, or all the teens needing Abercrombie. It is not even about something the man couldn't afford or get.

It is about you and me.

When we were baptized, we were clothed in Christ. And no amount of poverty can take that away. Get it? CLOTHED IN CHRIST! What did Paul say? "Dress yourselves in COMPASSION, KINDNESS, HUMILITY, GENTLENESS, and PATIENCE."

Don't take this parable out of its scriptural context. It is about you and me. And we need to know that admittance into the banquet is about more than showing up. It is about what we do with our baptismal garment, Jesus Christ.

The host is generous and expansive.

The host has prepared a sumptuous feast.

You have been invited.

So, what are you going to wear?

Twenty-Eighth Sunday in Ordinary Time (B)
Mark 10:17-30

Focus on the young man in the Gospel, not in an effort to understand HIM, but in an effort to understand yourself. But remember, no scripture passage should ever be used to give us quick answers. Rather the point is to give us WISDOM, which is different than answers! We need to ask, "what does this young man and Jesus' words to him ask of me?!"

Like the young man, we always want answers, don't we? And we want justification too. Unbalanced people want easy answers and even "religious" answers for their own ego enhancement.

Spiritually unhealthy people give religion a bad name because although they can quote Scripture and rattle off dogmas, they are always making demands, always laying on rules, always wanting to control others with their doctrine and law. They lack peace. They are argumentative. They are judgmental and even say things like, "If you do that you are going to hell!"

Spiritually healthy people, on the other hand bring peace, draw others to themselves, invite people into a relationship, show forth the face of Christ.

In the Gospel, Jesus was inviting the young man into a place of spiritual health and peace.

Like the young man, we are inclined to turn our spiritual life into a set of rules and theological abstractions. He was the product of the institutional religion of his day (the religion of the scribes and Pharisees) which was more about making demands than providing a relationship with God. It is a danger of all institutional religions. We are often very much a product of the institutional religions of our day.

If that young man were here today, he would have the same problem because we have even turned Jesus' message into reward or punishment. We have become rule-makers, umpires and judges. But Jesus, then and now, invites us into a relationship. "Follow me," is all he says. "Take a chance. Follow me (and see what happens)."

In my opinion, the young man had three things wrong with him, (and so do we!):

—The compulsion to feel justified:

("I'm keeping all the rules!")

—The compulsion to be right.

("I'm doing what I've been taught!")

—The compulsion to be in control.

("If I do this, I will be saved.")

None of us will ever be happy, ever be truly spiritual, unless we let go of all three compulsions. The young man, and we too, need to stop fixating on our own egos and our own hides. ("What do I need to do to be saved?")

The Christ question is rather, "What do I need to do to save others?"

The young man, and we too, are in search of righteousness and feeling good rather than the truth and love and a relationship with God. "Follow me," Jesus said.

The young man was looking for certitude, superiority and order. But Jesus never fed into that. Jesus never said, "You must be right, and here are the rules." All he said was, "Follow me."

Of course, if we follow Jesus, we will keep rules, but the rules are not first and foremost. The relationship is. And a relationship with Jesus is not about perfectionism but about participation in a mystery. Following Jesus and pursuing the relationship can be quite messy. It is not as cut and dried as keeping rules. But then any good relationship is messy.

To repeat, the Good News about this Gospel and about the gospel message in general is that it is not about being correct and neat and having all the answers or following all the rules. It is not about being justified. It is about being connected to Jesus.

Don't look at this Gospel for answers. Look at it for meaning. Like every Gospel, it is an invitation. "Follow me." Even though you might not know what that means. "Follow me." Even though you might mess things up. "Follow me." It is better than going away sad.

Twenty-Ninth Sunday in Ordinary Time (A)
Matthew 22:15-21

We are masters of deceit...masters of deflection. Which is probably why we dislike the Pharisees. They remind us of our worst selves. They seem always to be trying to trap Jesus or to validate their own failings. There are tons of examples of how we do this, but two come to mind.

For one, we all spend money unnecessarily, some more than others, but all of us to some extent. Whether it is a pallet of toilet paper at Walmart or a new car, we never say how much we spent. It is always, "I got a great deal. I saved this much." We need to deflect to pretend we are moral people. We never face the incrimination of St. Basil's quote, "The second coat in your closet belongs to the poor."

Another example of our moral posturing occurs with hot button social and political issues. You know what I mean. The so-called better Christians who are always carping about who is doing what in bed and ignore the fact that millions of people don't even have a bed.

The Pharisees were like that in today's Gospel. They tried to avoid their own guilt, their own legalism. They thought they had the perfect trap when they approached Jesus: There was a clear Jewish law against using graven images. So, they ask Jesus, "Is it lawful to traffic in coins that bear the image of the Emperor who claims to be divine? What do you say Jesus? Should we pay the tax? We need to use the Roman coin to pay the tax. And another thing Jesus, you have been proclaiming the kingdom of God for three years, but whose kingdom do you live in, really? Caesar's or God's. And how do you manage the dual citizenship Jesus? Do you pay the tax that is used to oppress the Jewish people?"

If Jesus says, "pay the tax," he is a sinner, breaking Jewish law, using a coin with a graven image. If he says, "don't pay the tax," he is a criminal by Roman law.

152

Jesus does answer, but it is not the answer as we have understood it for years. We have always interpreted his response as meaning we can have it both ways: we can get in bed with the political powers AND continue to be faithful. But we can't. Pay your taxes and say your prayers. But that is NOT what Jesus said or did.

"Show me the coin," he says. Jesus didn't carry such idolatrous currency around, but the Pharisees have got one handy. Isn't that interesting? He shows them to be the lawbreakers. He doesn't even have a coin. They are carrying the graven image around. He exposes their hypocrisy.

But then he goes even further. In their Book of Genesis, which all Jews knew well, it says clearly that God created everything, and that everything—earth and all its fullness—belongs to God. They knew that. It was fundamental to their whole law. In their desire to justify themselves and trap Jesus they forgot what was most basic to their faith: everything belongs to God.

He turns the trap on them and at the same time denies Caesar all power.

"Repay Caesar, what is Caesar's." He is not telling them they can have it both ways. Quite the opposite. He is telling them to take a stand. Caesar owns nothing! The coin is worthless.

In this Gospel, Jesus is giving new direction and renewed life to the whole world. Jesus is taking away all of Caesar's oppressive power. This Gospel (and the answer we thought Jesus gave) is revolutionary, even radical. Jesus is claiming all loving and life-giving power for his Father. And to the extent we allow the earthly powers around us to determine our response to life, to that extent we commit idolatry.

The image of Caesar was only on that worthless coin. But we bear the image of the true God. We are made in God's image. The spirit of God is breathed into our very souls. Jesus wasn't just after the Pharisees. The rug needs to be pulled out from beneath OUR game too. Jesus takes away all our defenses and pulls us out of our comfort zone so we can free-fall into the loving arms of our Father.

Twenty-Ninth Sunday in Ordinary Time (B)
Mark 10:35-45

Most of us probably smile at the naiveté of the disciples. Jesus asks them if they can drink his cup of sorrow, if they can share his baptism of suffering. We look at it with hindsight. We know it meant suffering and death. They were probably thinking, "Oh a little resistance from some people, a bit of anger from the powers that be...we can handle that."

And so they blithely answer, "We can do that." They completely missed Jesus' references to his real suffering, his real rejection, his very real death.

But as a matter of fact, they did do it. When the time came every single one, all of the Apostles were martyred for their faith in Jesus. Turns out they could do it.

I would offer that it is the same with us, and this Gospel is a reminder of the power we have in Christ Jesus.

Most of the time our reaction is the total opposite of that of the Apostles. We say, "I CAN'T DO THIS."

A woman lays terminally ill in her hospital room. Her adult son says, "I can't do this." He can't go in. He doesn't know what to say. He is terrified he will say something clumsy or stupid. And the rest of the family assures him he can do it. And he can. And he does. He walks in, he holds her hand. All he says is, "Hi Mom." And her failing eyes light up. He can do it.

A woman is at that crucial point in the delivery room. The pain becomes more than she can bear. "I can't do this," she says. But those around her assure her. "Yes, you can." And she does. And she brings a beautiful child into the world. She can do it.

He gets the diagnosis. It is devastating. His first thought is, "I can't do this." The surgery, the rehab, the treatment, the altering of his life. But with prayer and care and support, it all happens. He can do it.

154

The marriage break-up was anything but amicable. She hasn't gotten over his betrayal. He felt disconnected from her for years. The divorce is old, but the hurt still stings. And now their adult son asks them to come together to meet the woman he wants to marry. They are both anxious and still angry. They haven't spoken to one another except through legal proceedings. They both think the same thing, "I can't do this." But they love their son. And they do, in fact, do it. They can do it.

The high school student is overwhelmed. It doesn't matter whether it is a commitment to some sport or to some challenging academic program. He loses his initial enthusiasm. "I can't do it," he says. But with support from his parents or teacher or coach, he does do it. He can do it.

No matter whether it is a big thing or a small thing, a threat to our comfort or to our ego or our faith or our life. We can do it.

Discover in this Gospel the invitation to be more than you think you are...to do more than you think you can.

As I said, we usually react differently than the disciples when Jesus poses the challenge, "Can you drink the cup...can you immerse yourself in my baptism of fire?"

"No Lord, we can't. It is more than we can do." But in fact, Jesus never leaves us on our own, never turns us over to our weakness.

His life of humble service, his emptying of himself for others... it is all a promise. If we look to what is right...if we are motivated by generosity and compassion, if we open ourselves to the quiet presence of the Christ...then we can do it.

We can drink the cup. We can live his Baptism. We can bring good out of evil. We can transform darkness into light. It won't always be pretty; it will probably never be easy; and it certainly won't go smoothly...but we can do it.

Today, I am going to do something a little different. Rather than simply preach to you I am going to lead you through a reflection or meditation on this Gospel.

The ability to reflect or meditate is what makes us different than other animals. But, unfortunately, most people avoid reflection because they are threatened by what they might discover within themselves. Or maybe they have simply lost the ability to reflect because they have not done it for so long.

It was the pre-Christian philosopher Plato who said that a life not reflected upon is not worth living. Could that be why so many people feel worthless, aimless and without direction, bored? Maybe. But for now, simply give yourself over to it and see what emerges within you.

Bartimaeus is calling, calling, calling after Jesus. Like the beggar in the street outside the hotel in Chicago or Baltimore or wherever. You know, the one with whom you avoid eye-contact…as you either run away pretending not to hear or throw him a buck just to get him off your back. He is calling after Jesus.

I wonder whether Bartimaeus was asking to see for the first time in his life. Or was he asking to have his sight back? It doesn't matter. The verb used can mean either. But what do I need? Have I been blind all my life? Or was I OK once and now I need Jesus to heal me of this acquired blindness? It doesn't matter. What matters is Jesus is now the one doing the CALLING.

And then Jesus' disciples try to pretend that this is what they wanted all along. "Get up, he is calling you." I think that, up to that point, the followers of Jesus then, just as the followers of Jesus now, would have preferred that the beggar, the blind man, the problem, simply go away.

But then, Jesus is in charge of the drama here. "He's calling you," they say. If I were Bartimaeus I would have said, "No kidding Sherlock! I heard him. I'm not deaf!"

But maybe this is about me attuning my ears to the cries of those who are seeking Jesus. When I don't think I have anything to give...when I think I don't have time for this...when my own view is more important than the blindness around me. Maybe I need to see more as Jesus sees. To hear more as Jesus hears. There are people calling out all around me.

Maybe I'm the one who must say, "Get up. He is calling you."

And Bartimaeus didn't just drag himself over to Jesus, cowering in fear. No, he threw off his cloak...he SPRANG UP! He was in for the long haul.

And THEN Jesus asks, "What do you want?" Now that IS surprising. Don't you think Jesus knew what he wanted? I'm sure he knew. Is he just playing dumb? Of course not. What is necessary here is for the potential follower to articulate his heart's desire, to express what he really wants...to know what is really needed...to be open to what is really coming.

You know, when you can see clearly, there are no excuses.

Doesn't this compelling story give you and me the assurance that we can be healed of our inner blindness? Like Bartimaeus who threw aside his cloak and SPRANG UP, maybe we need to cast away whatever it is that we hide behind...whatever it is that we wrap ourselves in...whatever we use to shield ourselves from the harsh cold winds in our lives...whatever shields us from the demands Jesus makes...whatever it is that keeps us from springing up. We need to cast it aside and be naked before Christ and the world. Hiding behind nothing. Depending upon NO THING.

And THEN, Bartimaeus sees. It is a miracle. He sees.

But what happens next? Even though Jesus says, "Go your way," Bartimaeus does not go his way. He doesn't bound off only rejoicing in his ability to see. No, he follows Jesus. It is like he gives himself over to blindness again, blind faith this time, and follows Jesus. Now, even though he can see, he must trust his inner sight.

Isn't that what we all need? Not simply the ability to see but the inner sight, the only sight that can see God's love. That love that is stronger than any blindness...any sickness...any suffering...any rejection.

Isn't this the vision we need?

Thirty-First Sunday in Ordinary Time (A)
Matthew 23:1-12

Today's gospel message is doomed to be unpopular in our culture and society. "The greatest among you must be your servant." Right! "Whoever humbles himself will be exalted." That's not going to get much play. Almost everything we do and say points in other directions. We tell kids from the beginning to stick up for THEIR rights. We tell high school and college graduates to chart THEIR OWN course. We encourage one another to "march to your own drummer." What about community and the common good?

Obviously, most approaches have a good side to them. But they only work when they are tempered by life. I was thinking about some of the things we say that can be so NON-gospel. Consider some of these seemingly sage words.

Find YOUR Passion! Sounds great. Especially when some wise speaker says it to a group of college graduates. But life soon teaches us that discovering one's inner self is not so easy. It is a lifelong endeavor. It is often molded by the experiences of life. How many parents have discovered that the responsibility of raising a family often means their own desires take a back seat? Finding our own passion must never mean disregard for the needs of another. Yet that part of the advice is often left out of the commencement address.

Here is another one: Chart YOUR OWN course. But then, as we plan our life's journey, daily responsibilities get in the way of that romantic notion. A young woman feels called home to help care for a parent suffering from Alzheimer's and suddenly, her OWN course gets off track. A person working under a miserable boss must develop a whole new set of skills just to keep his job and his DREAM career course gets re-directed.

How about: March to the beat of your own drummer. That's great "self-help" book jargon. But what if your drummer is a bit off base? We all learn that we can make beautiful music when we play as part of an ensemble, and not everyone is a soloist. In Church we call it community.

158

And I like this one: Seek your own bliss! But in real life, happiness is elusive, and bliss is often hiding unless it is found in another's happiness: your spouse, your family, your child, your friends.

Today, Jesus is telling us that greatness and happiness are not discovered in merely FINDING ourselves, but in "losing" ourselves in the great tasks of life. We don't find contentment in our own wants but in our generosity, in our ability to help others find hope. It is not about exalting ourselves. Procuring simply our own satisfaction is ultimately demoralizing and disappointing.

NY Times columnist David Brooks articulates the problem when he says that we live in a cultural climate that preaches self as the center of a happy life. He points out that, as we age, as we live life, we discover that the responsibilities of life are at the center of a life well lived. He concludes that true life is only lived when the self dissolves into serious work and commitment that help us focus on others.

As followers of Jesus, we are not on a popular course. Some will think we are foolish. It is DOING good, not in recognition or seeking satisfaction that **we will** find happiness.

In the face of a rigid, religious culture, Jesus welcomed to his side the rejected and scorned and called out the self-satisfied leaders as hypocrites. Jesus washed the feet of his friends and taught them to do the same. Jesus says there is greatness only in losing ourselves and in the hard work of discipleship.

Speaking in the drab colors of the Pharisees and in the oppressive words of so-called religious leaders, even our own, is not what Jesus calls you and me to do. No, there must be a brightness in our work. But it is work. We are not about shining the light on ourselves. We are not about pursuing our own selfish goals. We must be about proclaiming the greatness of God, lifting the burdens of others and shining the light of the gospel in the dark places.

As we began today, we literally "sang up the saints." Although we do know something about these saints and the role they may have played in the faith community, we don't actually "remember" them. But today is officially called the Solemnity of ALL Saints. And that does include people you actually do remember or know.

As the Church opens the month of "remembering," I suggest you do something. If you don't get around to it today, it's OK, do it tomorrow or the next day. You have the whole month. I'm suggesting you make up your own list or litany of saints. You can put your list on a piece of scrap paper. (Maybe on your Facebook page...God knows it would be better than a lot of other stuff on Facebook.) It doesn't matter how you do it.

Write at the top, "I remember." Then start writing. Be thoughtful. You can use today's Gospel (the Beatitudes) as a guideline for who makes your list: someone who has touched your life; someone poor in spirit who showed you what has value; someone who was a peacemaker instead of a troublemaker; someone who was merciful and kind.

You get the idea.

Don't put someone on the list just because of their relationship with you. Don't worry about that. They might make someone else's list. This is YOUR Litany of Saints. (It might be good to think about whether you would make anyone's list. But then, that could be another homily.)

If you are young, your list will be shorter. If you are older, you will hopefully need a second sheet. You can go through your old address book...or maybe your old Christmas card list...or your email list. If you haven't updated them lately, all the better. This is about the past and the present.

Then keep this list. This list is you. And it is more than a list. Every one of the names is a marker of your own life. These are people who have inspired you, taught you (sometimes despite yourself). You remember because they have loved you, supported you.

Keep the list. It is really more valuable than your house or your car. Hang on to it. In fact, although you can't take anything with you when you leave this earth, I think you will be able to take this list.

Really. This list will comprise the ones waiting for you at heaven's gate, if/when you get there. In fact, if you get there, it will be because of this list. They will be the ones opening wide the gates and hanging the "Welcome Home" signs.

So today we celebrate and remember ALL the saints. Not just the official ones like Francis and Theresa and Joseph, but all the saints we have known and who have lived among us. They are the "Blessed" of the Gospel. They are the ones through whom God touches us and our world with humility and selflessness and generosity and forgiveness.

We make our list and we remember them. And don't doubt for a moment that, in the heart of God, they remember you too.

I have probably celebrated well over 2,000 funeral masses. On one hand, each one unique. On the other hand, many with real similarities.

The funeral where only four people were present, yet the power of the ritual spoke beautifully even among the empty pews.

Another where the sister of the deceased came to the parish carrying the cremated remains of her brother in a cardboard box.

There was one large funeral where the son told the story of his father's hands tucking him into bed as a child. As an adult, the son held those hands while his father lay dying after their estrangement of 30 years. Unnamed emotions hovered over the congregation that day.

There was the funeral of the man who held a gun to his own head in the driveway of the rectory and snuffed out his own life. Many years of depression had been hidden from public view but now, here were hundreds of people trying to understand the suicide of someone they thought they knew.

There was the funeral of the old man whose wife was angry at God because her husband of 55 years was gone from her before she was ready.

Such human stories form our faith. And the liturgy of the Church is meant to help us embrace the grand mystery of death.

Death is real, and we must celebrate each person's death with honesty and integrity. We must have the courage to tell the truth at funerals. Death is not hidden among the flower arrangements. Nor can we pretend it doesn't exist so as not to embarrass the living.

As so many families drift away from the rituals of the Church, the name "death" is also getting a face-lift. "Celebration of Life" has replaced the word funeral. Funeral homes became funeral chapels and then Family Life Centers and Gathering Rooms. People won't bring their children to calling hours for a dead grandparent yet think nothing of exposing them to the latest "haunted schoolhouse with four levels of terror and fear."

What are we thinking? We avoid anything that names the reality of death, while at the same time embracing bizarre behavior and attitudes. And this denial becomes more devastating than death itself.

But each year, here comes the Church, the community of faith, holding up the entire month of November, holding up the reality of death for all to see, holding up the mourning and loss that makes us human, holding up the memory of those who have preceded us in faith.

It is not because we are gruesome or morbid or wallowing in depression. It is because we are people of faith. It is because we believe in the Communion of Saints. It is because we know who we are. It is because, at some deep, even unexpressed level, we know what we are called to be.

Our lives are both precious and precarious. Today's Gospel parable makes it clear that we have only so much time to live lives that matter.

In the "old days" when I was in East Liverpool, Ohio, people still thought of the sacrament of the sick as the "last rites" and often put off the sacrament until it was too late or very near the end. We were on call at the hospital 24 hours a day. We would be called out at all hours, midnight, or 2 in the morning, or whenever, to minister last rites. Often family members would be there, and they would meet me in the hallway and say, "Oh Father, don't scare him. Just tell him you're making your rounds and want to give him a blessing." I would think to myself, "the guy is sick, not stupid. He knows Father doesn't make his rounds at 2 in the morning!" But it was the family who was scared.

In my 40 plus years as a priest, I have seen many people who were dying who had lived long lives. Others were so sick, and in such pain, that only death would release them. But the people who had the most trouble with death were teens and young people who thought they were invincible and older ones who felt that they had never done anything worthwhile in their lives. It was not so much death that frightened them. It was insignificance or the fear that they would die and leave no mark on the world.

For all of us, there is so much we want to do with our lives. But the many demands on our time and our desire for acquiring things derail us from making a true and valuable life, a life centered in love of family, a life lived with compassion for people, a life that finds fulfillment in contributing to the greater good of all, a life grown in awareness of God's presence.

In the end, the foolish virgins didn't get it right. This parable is unique to Matthew's Gospel. In Catholic tradition, the ten virgins are seen as images of the virginal Church with her heart set on God alone.

This parable is followed a little later in the Gospel with Jesus teaching that "whatsoever you do for one of these least ones, YOU DO FOR ME." It is the last judgment scene focusing on the works of mercy.

To all appearances the virgins are all alike. They are dressed for the wedding. They are where they need to be. Each has the lamp she was given (an image of our baptismal light). They all fall asleep. But only five were wise enough to bring oil. The oil represents loving deeds done in faithful witness. That's why the oil could not be shared.

There are some things that cannot be done for another. There are some things that cannot be given to another. There are some things we cannot TELL others. (Parents learn that lesson early on.) There are some things each of us must do for ourselves. And besides, the point of the parable is not about sharing. It is about being ready for the Lord, plain and simple. For the people who die unprepared or for the foolish virgins, would tomorrow be any better than the "tomorrows" we have all already had? Somehow, for the people who plan to get it right "tomorrow," tomorrow never comes.

This is about keeping our light burning all the time. It is about good deeds that light up our lamps. It is about treasuring and nurturing the free gift of faith we have been given. It is easy enough to be faithful once in a while, to celebrate Eucharist once in a while, to do good once in a while, to pray once in a while or when we are in trouble. The real challenge is to live for the long haul, not the instant gratification. Indeed, this Gospel is about what we will do today to light up our tomorrows.

Thirty-Third Sunday in Ordinary Time (B)
Mark 13:24-32

People love to obsess and hold forth about this Gospel, about the end times, about when and how. It has provided fodder for much ignorant and fundamentalist preaching in our churches, in an effort to control and scare people into being good. Moreover, when a tragedy occurs, like it did in Paris yesterday, it just feeds into that theory that sees God as meting out punishment and bringing the world to a cataclysmic end. In reality, such disasters are the result of human ignorance, anger and greed rather than about God throwing lightning bolts.

But when it really comes to the end times or the end of the world or the coming of the kingdom or the *eschaton*, as it is called, our true Christian tradition holds everything in balance.

In our tradition, there are two aspects to the coming of the kingdom. The first is called the "already" and the second is called the "not yet." Most of the time, when Jesus talks about the coming of the kingdom, he focuses on the "already," the kingdom has come…the kingdom is now. It is only rarely that Jesus focuses on the "not yet" aspect of the kingdom…the end times.

As I said, in Christian history, there have been those who have focused on the end of the world, the last days. But the best biblical scholarship and the best theology has always focused on the kingdom among us and our place in the kingdom. Isn't that what Pope Francis is urging us to do? Take care of the world you're in now. Be a church of mercy and forgiveness now.

Thomas Long in his book *Preaching from Memory to Hope* tells the story of a minister and his wife leaving church one evening. As they were heading to their car, they saw an elderly man lying in the parking lot with the man's wife bending over him. As the minister's wife made a call for an ambulance, the minister ran to the man's side to assure him that help was on the way.

The man looked up at the minister and said, "Charlie, please forgive me." The minister continued to comfort the man, "Don't worry; help will be here in a minute."

166

But the man persisted, "Charlie, please forgive me." The minister finally said, "I'm Sam, but really, help will be here soon."

The man was clutching his chest. It was clear he was not going to make it. And with all the life that was left in him, he grabbed Sam's arm and said, "Charlie, I beg you: forgive me." Sam simply said, "I do forgive you. I do forgive you."

Those were the last words that man heard. What Sam later learned was that the man had one son, named Charlie, and in an ugly argument years and years earlier, he had disowned his son, and hadn't spoken to him since.

Sam later wondered if he had done the right thing, but then realized how all this must have weighed on the old man's spirit. The man's dying wish was for forgiveness.

Today's Gospel isn't about projections and predictions. It is about the precious limits of our time now. It is about the kingdom in our midst now. It is about the forgiveness and reconciliation and peace that we can give one another now because Christ is already in our midst.

We often squander our time trying to justify our own self-righteous anger instead of reconciling with the lost and mending the broken. Let's not lose focus. The year is certainly racing headlong into its end. But November 29 is the first Sunday of Advent, the beginning of a new year for us in the Church.

Our Christian story does not have a scary ending. Our story is about an eternal now, a cosmic redemption, an invitation into God's future.

Really! What about the other nine? Have you ever wondered whether they got their leprosy back? Well maybe not exactly in those terms. But if they did, it would serve them right, after all. We want people to be grateful to us for what we do. We hate ingratitude. We keep score on people's gratitude toward us. We hate the attitude of entitlement that poisons our culture. And it is not something new.

Winston Churchill told the story about the little boy who fell off a pier into deep water. An older sailor, with no concern for himself, dove into the stormy water, struggled with the boy and brought him to safety. Two days later the boy's mother came to the same pier looking for the sailor. Finding him she asked, "Are you the one who dove into the ocean to save my boy?" "I am," he replied. The mother quickly demanded, "Then where's his hat?" (We know people like that. Churchill had a keen insight into human behavior.)

But all that being said, this Gospel is not so much about our gratitude. Neither is this Thanksgiving Day. We make it about us giving thanks, but it is more about God's unconditional love, God's unearned forgiveness, God's untold mercy, God's great abundance, God's healing grace.

This Gospel is one more example of that other Gospel we have trouble with. You know the one. "To those who have, more will be given." They all were cured of leprosy. But this guy, this Samaritan, this outsider got even more. He got the gift of faith.

I have a suggestion, when you say your grace today…when you offer your prayer of thanks to God, ask for "the more" for yourself and your family. God won't think you are ungrateful. He won't remove the blessings he has already given you. God will always give you "the more"—the gift of faith. That will be the life changer.

INDEX of NAMED REFERENCES

INDEX of NAMED REFERENCES (cont'd)

ACKNOWLEDGEMENTS

Thank you to the parishioners of St. Luke who inspired many of these homilies and to Mickey Fata for encouraging us to bring more of her brother's homilies to print.

A special thanks to Ursuline Ministries for its sponsorship of this volume, from the typing and editing assistance given by members of its leadership team and staff to funding for pre-publication expenses. From Ursuline Ministries: "Joe always had great affection and respect for the Ursulines, his first teachers, and we for him. He was a much-loved priest, colleague and friend we lost too soon, and supporting this book has been our great privilege."

And thank you most of all to Joe Fata, for leaving us an inheritance of grace, a legacy of love: "Those whom we love and lose are no longer where they were before; they are now wherever we are" (Saint John Chrysostom).

ABOUT THE AUTHOR

Father Joseph Angelo Fata was a priest in the Diocese of Youngstown for 48 years, serving as Pastor of St. Luke Parish (Boardman) for 28 of those years. He also served as Pastor of St. Joseph Parish (Mantua), and Associate Pastor of Our Lady of Peace (Canton) and St. Aloysius (East Liverpool). He was a founding member of the social justice organization ACTION (Alliance for Congregational Transformation Influencing Our Neighborhoods). He died on August 1, 2016 at the age of 74 after a long battle with cancer.

He always considered the celebration of Eucharist to be the heart of the life of the Catholic community and the key to maintaining the long tradition of the Church. The homilies and reflections in this book represent his convictions as a Catholic priest and preacher and his desire to serve, to lead and to inspire the people of God.

Volume 1 of "Mass to Mission" was originally published in 2015 and reprinted in 2019 concurrent with this publication of Volume 2. A collection of his poems and reflections, "Chronology of a Life Well Loved," was published posthumously in 2017, and in 2018 it was recognized with a Catholic Press Association Book Award. All of Fr. Fata's books are now available on Amazon.com for purchase.